The Power of the Seven

Darren Tyler

Published by Darren Tyler and Conduit Church
1642 Lewisburg Pike, Franklin, Tennessee 37064
Visit online at mylifegift.com

Published in association with Ivey Beckman Enterprises
iveyharringtonbeckman.com

Scripture quotations marked (NIV) are from the New International Version. Copyright © 1973, 1978, 1984, 2001 by Biblica, Inc. Used by permission.

Scripture quotations marked (MSG) are taken from The Message.® Copyright © 1993, 1994, 1995, 1996, 2000, 2001, 2002. Used by permission of NavPress Publishing Group

Scripture quotations marked (KJV) are from the Holy Bible, King James version.

Cover Design by Nick de Partee
Interior Design by Ryan Dunlap

Printed in the United States of America
IBSN # 979-8-6828985-4-1

Contents

This book is dedicated to my beloved Shannon.
You sacrificed so much for this book to be written.
It's my prayer that as you read these words you know
you are seen, you are wanted, and you are loved.

Discover your life gift.
Take the free quiz at:
mylifegift.com

Part I

Distinguishing the Gifts

"We have different gifts, according to the grace given to each of us. If your gift is prophesying, then prophesy in accordance with your faith; if it is serving, then serve; if it is teaching, then teach; if it is to encourage, then give encouragement; if it is giving, then give generously; if it is to lead, do it diligently; if it is to show mercy, do it cheerfully."

– Romans 12:6-8; NIV

Chapter 1

Dead Man Rising

"Readily recognize what he wants from you, and quickly respond to it."

– Romans 12:2; MSG

The Power of the Seven

BRIAN REDMON DROPPED DEAD in Conduit Church on a Sunday morning in March of 2014. When you grow up in a Charismatic church, as I did, here's the first thing that comes to mind when someone hits the floor: *No need to panic; they just got hit with the Holy Ghost.* But as good as worship was that Sunday morning, it wasn't that good. And the Holy Ghost doesn't turn your lips blue.

One of the things they don't prep you for in Bible college is what to do if someone drops dead during one of your church services. (It's possible a professor covered this in one of my courses, but I skipped class a lot.)

I froze for a second or two, waiting for the real pastor to arrive, but I was the guy. I felt sorry for the people who assumed I would know what to do. There was no time to learn on the job. Brian was going, going, and almost gone. And then the miraculous happened. The power of seven Life Gifts kicked in.

Historically, the seven I'm talking about are the gifts of prophecy, service, teaching, encouragement, giving, administration, and mercy. But as I've watched those with these gifts in action over the last few years, I've come to realize the persona of each gift is far more dynamic and lifechanging than I ever imagined. And the way all the gifts work together is far more intrinsic and powerful than we ever dreamed possible.

That's why I wrote *The Power of the Seven* and gave the seven gifts, defined and described in Romans 12, more relatable names:

Visionary (prophecy)
Collaborator (service)
Discerner (teaching)
Encourager (encouragement)

Imparter (peacemaking)
Guardian (administration)
Responder (mercy)

These new names aren't translations of the original Scripture. Instead, they are interpretations based on their original meanings in Greek. These seven supernatural gifts work miraculously together every day, just as they did that startling Sunday in the spring of 2014. Even now, thinking back on that day, it's remarkable how everything unfolded.

When Brian dropped to the floor, Kim Larocca promptly called 911. She didn't blink; she didn't wait for instructions. I had seen Kim in action when she fought for the life of her twelve-year-old son, who had a brain tumor. She's a fearless momma-bear **Guardian (administrator)**. When seconds count, you can count on Kim.

In a room full of people focused on the front of the room, Kim stood up and shouted, "Darren!" She was not afraid to interrupt me and speak up. We had just gathered the kids into the room for prayer, and Kim firmly instructed others to escort them out of the room. Brian's young daughters were among those children who were spared further trauma by not witnessing the intensity of saving someone's life. Kim's Guardian spirit ensured that.

Guy Roberts, an **Imparter (peacemaker)**, sensed the fear and uncertainty in the kids. He instantly took Kim's directive, gathered the children from the auditorium, and slipped out a side door. At the same time, Jim Henderson, another **Imparter** and our children's pastor, began comforting our kids. How kind is God to have a pair of nurturing Imparters working side-by-side in that tense moment? Guy and Jim were a double dose of peace in a situation that needed every bit of it. I can't think of a better team to be with scared children than those two men. They radiate peace. Our kids were in good hands.

If you're going to have a heart attack, crashing while standing next to Michelle Anderson is a good place to do it. Michelle is a longtime cardiac nurse with superior life-saving skills. She's also a **Visionary (prophecy)**. Michelle shoots straight without pulling any punches. She saw what was needed to save Brian's life and began telling others what to do—and fast.

David Christopher, a **mercy-filled Responder**, worked beside Michelle doing chest compressions like a boss. Along with the chest compressions, David, who leads from his heart, talked to Brian, telling him repeatedly, "You're going to make it; hang on. Your beautiful wife and children need you."

I'm not sure if Brian heard David, but the rest of us did. David was speaking to Brian, but his words reached us too. They were calming, reassuring. (David and I have traveled the globe together, and I made a mental note that I'm in good hands with him by my side.)

Sarah Dunlap, a medical professional who is an **Encourager (encouragement)**, rubbed Brian's feet to increase blood circulation. At the same time, she breathed prayers over him and those working to save his life. While David and Sarah were doing their thing, Sue Mohr, another **Encourager**, spoke comforting words to the frightened Redmon children.

Jeremy Hezlep, another **Imparter**, senses needs before he sees them. I've known him for most of his adult life, and he has always been that way. He sprinted to get the AED (Automated External Defibrillator). At that time, we held our church services in a public school, and public schools have AEDs. Jeremy grabbed the AED and brought it to Michelle, who knew exactly how to use it.

Jeremy was able to find that medical device in that gigantic high school because Donna Henderson, a **Guardian**, was in the room. Of course, she knew precisely where the AED was.

Joe Speno, a faithful and dependable **Collaborator (service)**, made sure the path was clear from the auditorium's front door where we were meeting. Several other Collaborators stood in the parking lot, waving in the ambulance and guiding para-medics inside, saving valuable seconds. Others moved cars.

Many other things happened that Sunday morning. Melissa Irwin, a **Guardian**, immediately offered to bring meals to the Redmon family. That Sunday was Melissa's first day to visit our church. What an introduction! But Guardians protect wherever they are, and Melissa immediately thought of the Redmon children and their mom. **Collaborator** Shannon Tyler and **Guardian** Deidre Phillips joined together to ensure that people's belongings made it back to them.

Jayna Christopher, another **Guardian**, did something that nobody but a Guardian would have thought to do—she docu-mented what happened, taking detailed notes. It's because of Jayna that my memories of that day are crisp. She protected the integrity of the experience.

What was this **Discerner (teacher)** doing? The Discerner gift allows me to detach from emotion and problem-solve in a crisis setting. I'm the pastor of Conduit, so the people in the room take their cues from me. If I panic, they panic. Like a duck, my feet were paddling a mile a minute under the water, but I was teaching calm and praying with the rest of the church on the surface.

The best thing I could do that day was to stay in my lane and let those with the other six gifts deliver a solution to a sig-nificant problem. I was teaching that the seven supernatural gifts of Romans 12 are the perfect God-designed response to any challenge the world throws at us. I had the microphone, but my microphone was only one-seventh of the solution—one tool in a cadre of God's powerful seven gifts.

As stressful as that Sunday morning was, a surreal calm saturated the room. We were watching the body of Christ in action, and even though we didn't have language for it, we felt the effects.

The entire episode, from when Brian dropped to the floor until the ambulance raced him to the hospital, lasted about fifteen minutes. It could have been pandemonium, but it was just the opposite because the seven gifts worked together. Much of what happened wasn't linear, but simultaneous. It was more like watching the parts of the human body work in unison rather than a successive checklist of things happening one at a time. It was problem-solving through fluid orchestration. It was the body of Christ fulfilling its purpose on a Sunday morning. It was the power of the seven demonstrating and validating God's best way to approach a challenge.

In the weeks and months that followed Brian Redmon's heart attack, those seven gifts continued to embrace the Redmon family. What do you call this? A church. Jesus called it His body.

In the interest of full disclosure, I do think we had one misfire that day. Brian's wife, Shelley, was at home that morning. Someone had to call her. Making a sensitive call like that would've come naturally to a Responder like David Christopher, but he was busy doing chest compressions. He randomly handed his phone to the person closest to him, an Encourager. We'll explore it later in the book, but an Encourager is high-octane joy, fast-paced, and typically not detail-oriented. The person who made the phone call spoke quickly, jumbled the details, and left Shelley with more questions than answers. That individual wasn't gifted to make a personal phone call about a medical emergency. It's nobody's fault; it was just an in-the-moment misfire.

I mention this misfire because we'll be looking at the seven gifts and the importance of deploying them in the right places at the correct times. After all, it matters. The person who made the call to Shelley is an amazing part of our church family, but the situation's emotional intensity was way out of his lane. The church needs to help members of the body of Christ know their own gifts and recognize those of others so that the seven gifts have full power.

Today Brian is thriving. The doctors at Vanderbilt told us that, without the AED, we would have lost him. And here's the bonus ending to the story: A year after his heart attack, Brian and Shelley received a beautiful surprise. With their eldest son heading to the Navy, they learned Shelley was pregnant! She gave birth to a perfect baby boy. He scampers around the church every Sunday, and I can't help but think that he wouldn't be here if it weren't for the power of the seven.

Brian has no memory whatsoever of that Sunday morning at Conduit Church. He barely recalls going to church that day. It does my heart good to know Brian's heart continues to pump on Sunday mornings and throughout the week. He is one of my close friends and a fellow Navy parent, each having a child in the nuke program. It's a bond like no other.

Although Brian Redmon's death-drop in our church is a dramatic instance of the seven gifts working together to solve a problem, it's just one incident on a long, ever-growing list forever inscribed on my mind and heart. The power of God's seven supernatural gifts is jaw-dropping—miraculous and yet humbling. When the body of Christ works in unison as God intended, the dead rise, the hungry eat, the broken heal, and mountains move—but no one gets a big head about it.

We could never accomplish such things without God; all of this is His idea. He handpicks a gift for each of us, and then we get to use our combined gifts to spread God's love. And it's an every-day-of-the-week thing, not just a once-in-while gig.

I love the way The Message phrases Romans 12:1-2:

> *"So here's what I want you to do, God helping you: Take your everyday, ordinary life—your sleeping, eating, going-to-work, and walking-around life—and place it before God as an offering. Embracing what God does for you is the best thing you can do for him. Don't become so well-adjusted to your culture that you fit in without even thinking. Instead, fix your attention on God. You'll be changed from the inside out. Readily recognize what he wants from you, and quickly respond to it."*

When I hear people talk about leaving the church and doing the Jesus thing on their own, it makes me sad. Not because I think they need to be sitting in a row every Sunday morning, but because when the church releases people to step into their giftings, we can—quite literally—change the world.

When we discover, develop, and deploy our God-given gifts, the world is a better place. Stuff gets done—and life is fulfilling, even fun. It's certainly not dull!

Get ready to discover your place in *The Power of the Seven*. Get ready to stop doing life as best you can on your failing strength and begin to energetically be the person God created you to be—someone who works in concert with others to accomplish fantastic stuff that matters on earth and in heaven. Get ready to know without a doubt that you belong. That you matter. That you are indispensable. That you are on earth for a purpose.

Your God-picked gift is already within you. It's time to discover it and see how God wants to use your gift because Jesus paid the ultimate price to give it to you.

Chapter 2

The Cost of Your Gift

This is why it says: "When he ascended on high, he took many captives and gave gifts to his people."

– Ephesians 4:8; NIV

IT'S NO ACCIDENT that there are seven supernatural gifts. Throughout Scripture, the number seven appears over and over again. It represents completion. It's God's perfect number. Whenever you see the number seven in Scripture, there's an underlying message of completeness. God created the world in six days, and on the seventh, He rested. He didn't rest because He was tired; God rested because there was nothing else to do. When you move from the Book of Genesis to the last book, Revelation, you'll also find it brimming with sevens: seven lampstands, seven spirits before God's throne, seven angels, seven seals, seven trumpets, seven churches, seven stars.

God also told Joshua to have the people of Israel march around Jericho seven times. On the seventh day, seven priests blew seven trumpets, and the walls came tumbling down. Those Jericho walls were a raw display of the power of the seven, but Jesus is the living proof. You see, in God's economy, seven adds up to getting stuff done.

PAYING THE ULTIMATE PRICE

If the power of the seven gifts working together doesn't motivate you to discover, develop, and deliver your gift, maybe the price Jesus paid for it will. Why? Because the seven gifts God gave the body of Christ to fulfill His mission on earth correspond with the seven places from which Jesus bled during his crucifixion. The number seven exemplifies the complete forgiveness the blood of Jesus purchased and (drumroll) the church's correlating gifts. Think about that as we take an up-close look at the crucifixion of Jesus.

First, Jesus bled from His forehead. The sharp, jagged thorns on the crown soldiers jammed onto Jesus' head ripped His scalp and brow. You were on His mind when this happened. Jesus had connected the dots of the hundreds of prophecies and knew what He needed to do. The blood from Jesus' head reminds us of the significant cost paid for the gift of teaching He gives Discerners. Those with this gift grasp what needs to be done, even when it seems too complicated to understand.

Jesus also bled profusely from his back. Roman soldiers used a torture instrument called a *flagrum*, which consisted of pieces of bone and metal attached to strands of leather. This picture of personal sacrifice reminds us that Jesus has our backs. Those with the gift of mercy, Responders, have our backs. They're not going anywhere—even when the going gets tough.

When the Roman soldiers pounded a seven-inch long spike into Jesus' right hand (likely hitting the median nerve), He bled, and the pain radiated throughout His body. The right hand, often described as the hand of strength, symbolizes that the gift of administration is an attribute that speaks of protecting the body of Christ, and naturally, Guardians do this.

Jesus also bled when a nail pierced His left hand. In Scripture the left hand of God speaks of His peaceful, giving nature. Through Imparters, the gift of giving flows from this hand into the body of Christ. Throughout His ministry, Jesus taught about giving money, but He gave His life for you on the cross.

When a seven-inch spike split the right foot of Jesus, He bled there too. The right foot symbolizes those who lead—Visionaries. Jesus took the first steps in and out of the grave, signifying the gift of those who naturally visualize what can and must be done—and charge forward.

Jesus' left foot also bled. The left foot works in concert with the right as the gift of service, moving alongside the body of Christ, balancing, and keeping up with the vision. The left foot ensures that the right doesn't stumble. It reminds us of Collaborators, who do this so well.

When a Roman soldier shoved a spear into Jesus' side, blood and water gushed out, which means our Savior's heart burst. That sacrifice was the ultimate manifestation of the gift of encouragement, reminding us that giving courage comes from the heart. Encouragers emulate this.

The seven places from which Jesus bled during His crucifixion paint a picture of the seven gifts He has given to us. Jesus paid the ultimate price to ransom us and give us gifts. When Jesus conquered death and the grave, He paved the way for these gifts. Jesus paid it all to give our gifts infinite value—and we are to steward them well out of gratitude for what He did. Together, we embrace the power of the seven interwoven gifts as the God-designed method for completing His will on earth. I love how The Message interprets Ephesians 1:11-12.

> *"It is in Christ that we find out who we are and what we are living for. Long before we first heard of Christ and got our hopes up, he had his eye on us, had designs on us for glorious living, part of the overall purpose he is working out in everything and everyone."*

Jesus paid the ultimate price so God could accomplish His glorious plan here on earth through us! Because of Him, we have the power of the seven!

THE BOUNTY OF WAR

The power of the seven gifts gains further momentum through the link to Ephesians 4:7. (Verse numbers in Scripture aren't inspired, but it's not lost on me that verse seven makes a connection between Jesus and the seven gifts of Romans 12.)

In the Ephesians passage, the Apostle Paul stated, "Grace has been given to each of us as Christ apportioned it." The Message places this spin on Ephesians 4:7: "Out of the generosity of Christ, each of us is given his own gift."

Ephesians 4:8 goes on to say, "When he ascended on high, he led a crowd of captives and gave *gifts* to his people" (4:8). Paul was quoting Psalm 68:18, which speaks of a king returning from battle. The imagery evoked is of a king who went into battle to rescue his people from a neighboring enemy. A king in those days (think David) did not watch from a distance. He led from the front—sword drawn—and fought alongside his men. The blood of soldiers paid for the bounty of war. Upon their return, soldiers paraded down the main thoroughfare, followed by those the king had freed from slavery. And a good king shared the bounty with his people by giving them gifts.

Paul was comparing what Jesus did in setting us free from sin to what a king would do to free his people from bondage. Jesus, in His triumphant return from battle, gave us—the body of Christ—gifts. He paid for those gifts with the blood from His body.

Paul also evoked the imagery of a body in Romans 12. That's not a coincidence. When I think of Jesus' physical body, I can't ignore that, in death, He offered it so that we could become His body here on earth. "You are the body of Christ," Paul said in 1 Corinthians 12:27. The pronoun "You" in this verse is plural, as in "you and I together" are the body of Christ.

When Paul used body references in the same paragraph as the seven gifts of Romans 12, he said something profound but straightforward. Your gift is your part of Christ's body, and it is most powerful when working in tandem with the other gifts. That's dynamic—and prophetic. You see, God wants the body of Christ to use the seven gifts listed in Romans 12 to impact the world! The term "body of Christ" isn't just a metaphor; it's God's method for getting things done on earth. It's God's delivery mechanism by which we, His representatives, deliver His grace to our homes, our communities, and the world around us.

Jesus is the head of the church. The body implements the ideas of the head. The seven gifts listed in Romans 12 are the power to fulfill the ideas of Jesus. They are indeed the answer to the most momentous prayer Jesus ever prayed: "Thy will be done on earth as it is in heaven."

Paul intentionally grouped these seven gifts in Romans 12 because their God-given power flows through unity, not isolation. Through interdependence, not independence. Through cooperation, not competition. And holding it all together? The elasticity of love. Love, my friend, is what keeps the body of Christ together. It's flexible, spiritual super glue.

Now that you understand what your gift cost Jesus, it's time to get smart about spiritual gifts because knowledge plays a significant role in the power of the seven gifts of Romans 12.

Chapter 3

Don't Be an Idiot

"Now about the gifts of the Spirit, brothers and sisters, I do not want you to be ignorant."

– 1 Corinthians 12:1; KJV

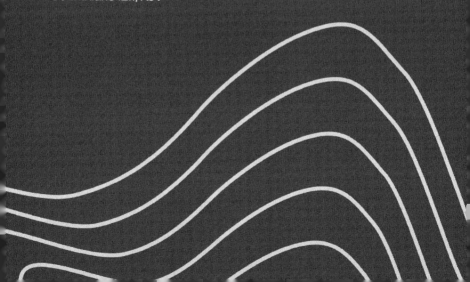

WHEN MICHAEL SCOTT, the boss in the sitcom The Office, asked employee Dwight K. Schrute, "What's the most inspiring thing I ever said to you?" Schrute quickly replied, "Easy. 'Don't be an idiot.' Changed my life. Whenever I am about to do something, I think *Would an idiot do that?* And if they would, I do not do that thing."

The Apostle Paul gave the same advice to us. When it comes to spiritual gifts, don't be ignorant. Don't be an idiot (1 Corinthians 12:1). Sadly, I did not heed that advice for much of my life.

I grew up in a Pentecostal church. One Sunday, I invited a friend to church on a day that (with no advanced notice) featured tongues and interpretation. For some reason, that always seemed to happen on the day I invited a friend. *Why today, Stella? Why today?*

Folks filing down front for healing often followed a tongues-and-interpretation service. There were "catchers" there to ensure those receiving prayer avoided injury while falling to the ground—a.k.a. *being slain in the spirit*. My whispered conversation with my stunned friend went something like this:

Me: "No, man. She's not dead. She has been slain in the spirit."
Friend: "OK, but you just said, 'slain.' Do you know what that word means?"

If you've never waded in that stream of Christianity, you have no idea what I'm talking about. I feel simultaneously sad and relieved for you. But back then, I thought of the gifts of the spirit as ethereal, desirable—and utterly embarrassing. They made me feel torn and tense, so it was much easier to tap out. I didn't scrap the enterprise entirely as much as I just ignored it. I remained ignorant. I was an idiot.

It took me a while, but when I did wise up, well, my whole world lit up like the porch of a redneck who leaves their Christmas lights on all year long. And I want the same for you.

UNDERSTANDING THE THREE DIFFERENT GIFT SETS

If you've ever taken a spiritual gifts assessment, you've likely engaged one that blends the twenty-one gifts listed in 1 Corinthians 12, Ephesians 4, and Romans 12 into one list. The results designate "your gift."

If you haven't participated in one of those assessments, they're the Christian version of a DISC Profile evaluation, a Myers-Briggs analysis, or "which Star Wars character are you?" You answer a set of questions about your personal preferences and presto! You learn who you are and which spiritual gift you have.

The results of spiritual gifts assessments tell you whether you're an evangelist, an administrator, an apostle, someone gifted for serving, etc. Once you get these results, you're assigned your spot in the church.

The intentions of such assessments are noble. No church needs a prophet in the nursery. ("Pastor, Sue is singing nursery rhymes about the Apocalypse.") Nor do we need an evangelist in the parking lot. ("Pastor, we can't get cars parked because Tom keeps doing altar calls!")

But here's the problem: Ephesians 4, 1 Corinthians 12, and Romans 12 are three separate lists. They are three distinct categories with three different purposes. By conflating the three sets of gifts into one comprehensive list and then picking one gift for each person, these assessments fall short of connecting any believer to full-power potential. Just in case you think I'm making this up, read what Paul wrote about spiritual gifts in 1 Corinthians 12:4-6.

"There are different kinds of service, but the same Lord." (This references the gifts of Ephesians 4:5.)

"There are different kinds of gifts, but the same Spirit distributes them. (This references the gifts of 1 Corinthians 12:4.)

"There are different kinds of working, but in all of them and in everyone it is the same God at work." (This references the gifts of Romans 12:6.)

Paul described three categories. Each category not only aligns with an individual member of the Trinity, it also aligns with the three different lists of gifts in Ephesians 4, 1 Corinthians 12, and Romans 12. Biblically speaking, to arm believers to light up the world for God, each believer has access to each list.

- Ephesians 4:5 says that Jesus calls some people to be the gifts listed there. (There are different kinds of service, but the same Lord.)
- 1 Corinthians 12 tells us that the Spirit distributes "them" (plural) to you (singular), indicating that we each *could operate* in more than one of those gifts. (There are different kinds of gifts, but the same Spirit.)
- Romans 12 tells us that *every single one of us has one of the gifts listed there*. (There are different kinds of working, but the same God at work.)

Translation? Some of us will be called by Jesus to be one of the gifts from Ephesians 4. And, from time to time, each of us has access to the manifestations of the Holy Spirit in our lives (1 Cor. 12). And all of us have a specific gift from Romans 12 given to us from God the Father.

Simply stated, the gifts from Ephesians 4 are *appointed*. The manifestations of 1 Corinthians 12 are *anointed*. The gifts of Romans 12 are *pinpointed*.

Understanding the purpose of each gift set means you can discover, develop, and deliver God's gifts in the way He has designed you to do it. The Designer is the Definer, and He has defined some fantastic ways for you to partner with Him in His kingdom work on earth. Let's look at each category.

Appointed Gifts: Ephesians 4

The gifts listed in Ephesians 4 are "appointed" by Jesus to "prepare people to do the work of the ministry." These are gifts given by Jesus to the body of Christ. He's appointing someone to do something, not to be someone. This gifting is a call to be answered, an appointment to be accepted.

The appointment is quite specific in Ephesians 4: "Preparing you to do the work of the ministry." The job of a pastor isn't to gather people so the pastor can do the ministry; it's quite the opposite. The pastor's job is to lead those gathered to go and do the work of the ministry.

God does not call everyone to be a pastor or an apostle. But the church needs them for preparation in the same way an army needs drill instructors. This appointment is not a glamorous gig, but an army can't function without it.

Anointed Gifts: 1 Corinthians 12

We learn in 1 Corinthians 12:4, "There are different kinds of gifts, but the same Spirit distributes them." There are spiritual gifts in 1 Corinthians 12 that are directly tied to the Holy Spirit. They are distributed by the Holy Spirit. Being anointed with oil and the presence of the Holy Spirit is a theme repeated throughout the entire Bible. These are gifts that are manifest by the anointing of the Holy Spirit.

In this passage, the message is clear: "to each one the manifestation of the Spirit is given for the common good." 1 Corinthians 12:7. A manifestation is an event that shows or embodies an abstract idea. It's the unveiling of something once hidden. The gifts of 1 Corinthians 12 are moments when the Holy Spirit manifests and makes something previously foggy crystal clear. The word "manifest" comes from a Greek root word that speaks of unveiling something. Think of it as wiping the fog off a mirror to get a better look.

All Christians have access to the gifts described in 1 Corinthians 12, but the Holy Spirit distributes them. That the Holy Spirit distributes them (plural) to each one (singular) means that more than one of these gifts might manifest in you throughout your life as you follow Jesus.

When my friend Mark stands before a crowd in Pakistan and proclaims, "Jesus is Lord, not Allah!" it's incredibly helpful when someone in the audience rises out of a wheelchair. The Word of God is confirmed when someone who comes to the event blind goes home able to see. It's what Mark 16:20 refers to when the Gospel writer penned that God will "confirm the Word with signs following."

These gifts are not parlor tricks or superpowers. Paul said they are "for the common good." They're an operation of the Spirit for a specific moment for a particular purpose—the common good of those present.

In 1 Corinthians 12:11, we read, "All these are the work of one and the same Spirit, and he distributes them to each one, just as he determines." If you want to see these kinds of miraculous gifts manifested, follow Jesus' command to go into all the nations and make disciples. These signs will follow you.

The gifts Paul spoke of in 1 Corinthians 12 are for the common good of the church. Some translations use the word "profit." These are gifts that are a manifestation through one person to benefit everyone.

To profit means to leave with more than you came with. These gifts deliver that. If you were sick, you go home with healing. A word of wisdom gives you more understanding than when you began. And so on. That's the heartbeat of appointed gifts.

PINPOINTED GIFTS: ROMANS 12

In Romans 12, we discover gifts that are "in accordance with the faith God has distributed to each of you." The seven gifts designated in Romans 12 are the pinpointed gifts God gives to each of us. He gives each of us a single, particular gift by His grace. These pinpointed gifts are not something we should hoard; God entrusts us to deliver our gift to others.

God wrote your Romans 12 gift into your DNA. This gift pinpoints who you are and reveals your purpose for your time on earth. Your Romans 12 gift is not God calling you to *do something* but to be someone.

Romans 12 gifts are for the unity of the body of Christ. Paul used the metaphor of a body with members together. Each member has a purpose. Knowing your purpose promotes unity for the common goal manifested through the head (Jesus). Pinpointed gifts give us individual focus to ensure overall strength and effectiveness in the body of Christ.

A TRINITY OF GIFTS: ROMANS 12

In 1 Corinthians 12:4-6, we find clarification about all the spiritual gifts:

> *"There are different kinds of gifts, but the same Spirit distributes them. There are different kinds of service, but the same Lord. There are different kinds of working, but in all of them and in everyone it is the same God at work."*

Did you catch that? All three members of the Trinity are mentioned here. Jesus distributes the gifts of service listed in Ephesians 4. The Holy Spirit distributes the manifestations of the Spirit noted in 1 Corinthians 12. God the Father distributes the working gifts of Romans 12.

Each member of the Trinity interacts with us in a unique and needful way. And each member of the Trinity distributes gifts through each of us. When we recognize that God has these three categories of gifts, with three distinct purposes, it dispels ignorance and opens up a whole new world of possibilities.

Simply put, some of us will be appointed to prepare others to do the work Jesus wants to accomplish in this world (Ephesians 4). When the Holy Spirit chooses, He can manifest Himself in us from one or more of the gifts of 1 Corinthians 12. And finally, the Father has given each of us a specific gift chosen from the seven pinpointed gifts. Each of us has a supernatural natural way of being in this world.

DESIRE THE GREATER GIFTS

Paul closed out 1 Corinthians 12 by asking, "are all apostles, are all pastors?" Of course, the answer is *no*. Then he said something profound: "Now eagerly desire the greater gifts." That's an intriguing statement given Paul's mandate that believers not be ignorant about spiritual gifts. And since Paul wasn't one to pull punches, we must answer this question: What are the greater gifts?

When you look at those closing verses (27-30), Paul referenced gifts from 1 Corinthians 12 and Ephesians 4, but not those listed in Romans 12. What do 1 Corinthians 12 and Ephesians 4 have in common? They are the more visible gifts, the flashy ones. Prophesying, speaking in tongues, and being an apostle are the gifts that get the most headlines.

But what did Paul point to as the greater gifts? It's evident to me that the greater gifts we should desire are those showcased in Romans 12. These gifts are greater because God chose one *specifically for each person*. These gifts are greater because God designed them to be in play every single day of your life. They require no special training or permission. They are woven into the very fabric of who you are.

The Power of the Seven is about the seven gifts revealed in Romans 12, which are so beautifully supernaturally natural. So natural that you might not recognize yours as a gift, yet so supernatural that those who don't have your gift look at you and wonder *How does she do that?* That's the supernatural natural element of the seven gifts of Romans 12.

I hope that by the time you finish reading *The Power of the Seven*, you'll discover your Romans 12 gift, know how to develop it, and begin delivering it to the world. You're already a step ahead of most Christians because you've followed Paul's advice—you're not ignorant of spiritual gifts. You, my friend, are not an idiot. And in this world, that's no small thing.

Chapter 4

You Are Indispensable

"It is in Christ that we find out who we are and what we are living for. Long before we first heard of Christ and got our hopes up, he had his eye on us, had designs on us for glorious living, part of the overall purpose he is working out in everything and everyone."

– Ephesians 1:11-12; MSG

The Power of the Seven

Y OU ARE ONE-SEVENTH OF THE SOLUTION to any problem the enemy throws at the world. One-seventh might sound inconsequential, but is there an inconsequential tire on a car? Is there an irrelevant blade on a helicopter? Of course not; each is indispensable! And so are you. You aren't a solo act; you're a specifically chosen and purposefully designed part of the answer to the most meaningful prayer Jesus ever prayed: "Father, ... your will be done on earth as it is in heaven" (Matthew 6:10).

You've repeatedly heard the axiom, "God has a plan and purpose for you," so perhaps its punch has been diminished. But here's the electrifying link you may have missed: That purpose isn't just about what you do on earth; it's about who you are. God didn't just create a physical body for you; He crafted your innermost being. He made the you that will go on long after your physical body stops working. When the Psalmist wrote that God "wove together your innermost being," he wasn't talking about your spleen. As miraculous as it is to create a sternum, it's incomprehensible that God created the you that makes you who you are.

These days, scientists can grow a human ear on the back of a mouse. (Feel free to Google that; however, be forewarned you can't unsee it.) But the world's sharpest scientists fueled by unlimited funds can't grow you on the back of anything. Only God has proven capable of creating the unique you. Of all the things He could have made, God created you. Don't you want to know why?

Mark Twain once said, "The two most important days in your life are the day you were born, and the day you find out why."[1] Personality profiles, such as Meyers-Briggs, DISC, and Ennea-gram, are tools that reveal *how* you're wired. The problem is, they don't tell you *why*. Romans 12 does, which sets it apart as more than just an exercise in psychology. The difference between those personality profiles and Romans 12 is that God gives you both the ability to know your personality and the power to become who He has designed you to be. You don't have to go through life winging it. There's a purpose for your life that fits how God wired you—and power to help you live it well.

By God's design, you're a unique, living, breathing gift—and when you unite with other Christ-followers, together, we become the answer to the most meaningful prayer Jesus ever prayed. How do I know this? Romans 12:5-8 lays out the seven gifts and reveals that each of us has one:

> "*so in Christ we, though many, form one body, and each member belongs to all the others. We have different gifts, according to the grace given to each of us. If your gift is prophesying, then prophesy in accordance with your faith; if it is serving, then serve; if it is teaching, then teach; if it is to encourage, then give encouragement; if it is giving, then give generously; if it is to lead, do it diligently; if it is to show mercy, do it cheerfully.*"

Paul compared these seven gifts to parts of a body. Each body part is different but connected to the shared mission of accomplishing what the head wants. Your gift represents the specific body part you represent. With this metaphor, when you discover your God-given gift, you learn the purpose for your life—the why of your birth. How cool is that?

Only in unison are we the body of Christ. Alone no one is the hands and feet of Jesus; together, we are. And what does a body do? Whatever the head desires. Jesus chose to accomplish His ideas on earth through us working together. Jesus could make it rain sandwiches. But He decided to feed the hungry through people like you and me.

In describing these seven gifts of Romans 12 using the body metaphor, we see that operating in unity brings the will of Jesus to earth. Three out of seven gifts might crawl through a problem, while five out of seven gifts could limp along. Six out of seven is an almost solution. But seven out of seven gifts working in union wields all of the dynamic elements of Jesus on earth, which is God's plan!

YOUR PLACE IN GOD'S WILL

Jesus chose His body—all of it—to accomplish His will on earth as it is in heaven. That's why you are indispensable to the mission of Jesus on earth. Sure, Jesus could've chosen to accomplish His mission without you, but He didn't. He chose you to be part of His mission. When you reject, ignore, or remain ignorant of the gift He wants to deliver to and through you, someone doesn't receive your much-needed gift.

Romans 12:1-2 reveals how to ensure you are part of delivering God's will on earth:

> "Therefore, I urge you, brothers and sisters, in view of God's mercy, to offer your bodies as a living sacrifice, holy and pleasing to God—this is your true and proper worship. Do not conform to the pattern of this world but be transformed by the renewing of your mind. Then you will be able to test and approve what God's will is—his good, pleasing and perfect will."

If you are anything like me, pondering God's will immediately leans toward doing stuff. Think about the prayers you've prayed for God to show you His will: where to attend college, whom to marry, what career to pursue, and so forth. Sure, that stuff matters. However, the God-given gift of who you are can serve as a guide for what you do—and it requires the transformation the Apostle Paul urged in Romans 12:1-2.

That heart-to-life transformation enables you to discern His will for your life—and it links directly to the specific Romans 12 gift He entrusted to you. His will for you is to be the person He created you to be—to feel in sync with a life track because it feels like it fits you. Stepping into who God designed you to be is freeing! It flings open the doors of your life. Proverbs 18:16 puts it this way, "your gift will make room for you."

So how does that play out? Romans 12:3 tells us:

> *"For by the grace given me I say to every one of you: Do not think of yourself more highly than you ought, but rather think of yourself with sober judgment, in accordance with the faith God has distributed to each of you."*

Inebriated people have one thing in common: they believe things about themselves that are not true. It's called "liquid courage," not "liquid wisdom." Thinking about yourself "with sober judgment" means believing the truth about yourself. I can't think of a better biblical definition of humility—*believing the truth about yourself.*

"Do not think yourself more highly than you ought" is wise counsel. As you read the seven gifts' descriptions in the upcoming chapters, you might find yourself wanting a different gift. Or, you might find yourself wanting to shun the one God entrusted to you. Those warped perspectives about your God-given gift are versions of thinking more highly of yourself than you ought.

I once heard Bob Goff say, "Every day I wake up, I want to be the next most humble version of Bob." I like that. It's how you and I grow into our gifts—in increments imperceptible by day but undeniable by year.

God didn't send us a manual; He sent us Immanuel, God with us. The Word became flesh and dwelt among us. We have

40

the Holy Spirit as a personal guide. Seeking treasure with a map is one thing. Seeking treasure with the one who hid it is quite another. The journey to discovering your gift doesn't stop once you have found it; that's just the beginning, so please don't get frustrated or obsessed as you seek to discover your God-given gift. You aren't seeking the gift; you're seeking the Giver of the gift. God will make your gift clear to you.

My friend Scott Sauls once tweeted, "We must preoccupy ourselves less with being like Jesus and more with simply being with Him. For when we've been with Him, we will become like Him. The fruit of the Spirit is caught, not achieved."[2]

Prioritize God's presence in your life. Jesus promised, "I will not leave you as orphans; I will come to you" (John 14:18). Daily spending time with Jesus is your life key. Offer your life to Him. And then, "you will be able to test and approve His will for your life" because your core desires will match His.

Psalm 37:4 tells us, "Take delight in the Lord, and he will give you the desires of your heart." (NIV). The Bible promises that a heart delighting in Him will have desires inspired by Him. To put it in a more modern vernacular: First, delight yourself in Him. Then follow your heart.

I can hear the retort: "But Darren, the Bible says that the heart is wicked and deceitful above all things." Yes, the Scriptures state that. And "follow your heart" is terrible advice if you're not in Christ, daily delighting in Him. Like you, I have followed my unsubmitted heart down some dumb paths. However, the prophet Jeremiah didn't stop with stating how terrible the heart is. He went on to say, "The Lord searches and knows our heart and mind." That's part of Immanuel, God with us. He leads you with your heart.

Part of the new covenant is that God will remove your heart of stone and replace it with a heart made of flesh (Hebrews 8:10). As a result of that new covenant, God will "write His laws on your heart and mind." His laws are His will. The idea being communicated is you no longer need a priest to tell you God's will for your life.

To know God's will, submit your heart to Jesus, delight in Him. God will use your fully submitted heart to lead you. When you find yourself thinking about something, and it makes your heart swell up, pay close attention. God may be writing His will on your heart.

Romans 12:3 offers direct guidance about the link between your heart and your gift: "...in accordance with the faith God has distributed to each of you." The faith isn't in your gift; it's in the Giver of the gift. And faith in the Giver of the gift gives you the power to be who God designed you to be.

The gospel is unique because it tells us the truth: Because we are toxic, nothing short of the death of the Son of God could save us. But the gospel also says that the Son of God loved us so much He died for us. The gospel explains that Jesus loves and accepts you just the way you are—and that He cherishes you too much to let you stay that way.

Here's how that truth lands. Yes, you were broken and without hope. And, yes, you are loved and infinitely valuable. The more you take that into your soul, the more your heart is softened. That gives you self-confidence exclusive only to Christianity.

Do you see how unique that is? The gospel gives you the power not to think more highly or lowly of yourself than you should. It also gives you the ability to believe the truth about yourself. Only the gospel of Jesus can address both extremes and enable you to think of yourself as Jesus thinks of you. The gospel doesn't command you to be humble; the gospel empowers you to be humble. The gospel doesn't command you to love yourself; the gospel empowers you to love yourself.

I'm convinced that's why the first eleven chapters of Romans explain the gospel's entirety in intricate detail. A heart that is fully submitted to and delighting in that gospel is one whose desires will lead you well.

Jesus allowed soldiers to pierce his heart so that your heart could be transformed. Take that truth deep inside yourself daily. Embracing a God that good means you can trust that whatever gift He has entrusted you to deliver is perfect for you.

With that at the forefront of your mind and heart, absorb the next seven chapters. In each, you'll meet someone whom God has entrusted with a specific gift and learn how that individual is changing the world by delivering it. You'll also meet a Bible character who serves as the mentor for that gift.

You'll discover your specific gift and recognize what an honor it is to be part of God's plan to save the world by lighting up the world for Him in your unique way. Sure, you'll spot traits of yourself in each gift as you read through the next seven chapters, but one of those gifts will speak to you more than the others. You'll think, *that sure sounds like me*. And your heart? Maybe it'll skip a beat. It is, after all, God's will, written on your heart.

Part II

Discover Your Gift

"God has given each of us a gift from His great variety of spiritual gifts. Use them well to serve one another."

– 1 Peter 4:10; NIV

The Power of the Seven

Chapter 5

The Visionary

"If your gift is prophesying, then prophecy according to your faith."

– Romans 12:6; NIV

GERALD LAFLEUR STOOD ON A STENCH-HEAVY, trash-strewn street and saw hungry, illiterate Haitian children void of hope; children whose heads were always down as if their bodies viscerally knew they had no future. *Why bother looking ahead to nothing?*

Gazing at those children, Gerald saw something he couldn't shake. He saw himself. He had grown up on the rough streets of Port-Au-Prince as one of five children born to a mother who did her best to care for him and his siblings. Gerald's mom did whatever she could to make sure her kids stayed in school with his father long gone. Like most Haitian kids, he was too poor to afford both food and school, so he often went days without eating.

But Gerald's mom was militant about his education. She would tell her hungry son, "If you eat your books today, tomorrow, your life will be better." She was casting a vision for him. She was teaching her son to push through present suffering to flourish in the future. She died when Gerald was still a teen. She never experienced in reality what her vision for the future saw so clearly then. But her dream was strong enough to live beyond her.

In Haiti, "making it" is often defined as getting to any place other than Haiti. And thanks to his mom, buried not far from where he stood that sweltering summer day in 2004, Gerald Lafleur had gotten out. He had made it and was pastoring a church on the neighboring island of Antigua. He was married to his beautiful wife, Elsa, and they had two healthy sons who were enjoying a life most Haitians can't even imagine, let alone attain.

So why was Gerald back on the streets of Haiti? Because the eyes of his Visionary heart could see what others could not: a flourishing future rising out of the dirt and despair of suffering today.

Sure, there are millions of children in Haiti scraping-out life in the worst of conditions. To the average person, Haiti is too far gone to have a future. It's not that the economy is devastated; there's no economy to devastate. Haitians live a sustenance existence born out of a rebellion long forgotten by the rest of the world. Gerald's ancestors were brought to Haiti as slaves 400 years earlier. When they overthrew their French captors, they were left to survive a life they didn't want on an island they didn't choose. Today, Haiti is the poorest country in the Western Hemisphere with the majority of her residents existing on less than two dollars a day.

Haiti has what is known as a shadow economy. The second-largest source of income is from ex-pat Haitians, sending money back to their families. It's easy to send money; what's hard is to send yourself, especially if you can't see any point in returning.

But Gerald saw a point. He didn't see what Haiti was; he saw what she could become. It's not that Gerald could predict the future; it's that he could envision a future and then make it happen.

When I first joined Gerald in Haiti, I saw hopelessness. I had been to other countries and felt the sting of extreme poverty, but Haiti is different. There's a poverty that's both systemic and generational. The electricity is off from 4 a.m. until nightfall every day. Plastic trash covers so many streets they appear to be made of it. Sewage fills the rivers and streams that are used for laundry, washing cars, and drinking. It took generations to unfold and will take more to overcome.

Blame it on the system. Blame it on corruption. Blame it on sin. The truth? I don't know whose fault it is, but I know it's not a five-year-old's doing. Even if it were only for the children, someone had to do something. Still, where would we even start to make a difference?

That's the wrong question. Here's the right one: Where will the Visionary start? Hitch your wagon to that horse, because the Visionary is going places.

Gerald looked into that community with eyes far keener than mine. He saw the great beyond. Romans 12:6 tells us that if your gift is prophesying (Visionary), then prophecy according to your faith. That's a glimpse into how this gift is delivered. A Visionary like Gerald Lafleur doesn't move forward according to the existing circumstances but according to his faith. The reality was rocky and uncertain. Gerald could see past all that and envision a school, a home for abandoned children, a church, a health clinic, and a feeding program. The circumstance was despair. But Gerald saw hope. Circumstance saw impossible, but Gerald, seeing with a heart crafted by God, could see "I'm Possible." He saw the seemingly insurmountable as an expansive opportunity.

For a Visionary, this mindset is almost visceral. It's just what Visionaries naturally do. They see injustice and fix it. Money, buildings, and land are all only tools to be utilized. Back then, if you had asked Gerald where the money was going to come from, he would've had no idea. It's not so much that it was beside the point as it was just another mountain to be climbed. It didn't occur to Gerald that he might fail. This world's systems were beating the Haitian kids to a pulp, and someone had to do something about that. To Gerald, his involvement was nonnegotiable. He was in it to win it.

"You don't wait until you have everything to start. If you do that, you'll never get anything done," Gerald told me. "There's no way to know how we will finish; sometimes, you can only know how you will start."

That's the voice of a Visionary. Lafleur didn't wait for provision or permission. He just started moving forward.

The feeding program started with fifteen kids who sat in the tiny living room of Pastor Rodrigue Moline while his wife cooked for them. The school fees for those kids were paid as well. It was basically, "OK, I'll sponsor these three, and you take those two. Philip will sponsor that one, and a few more friends will sponsor the rest." That's literally as much thought as went into it.

It wasn't easy. None of it was. Within a year, that little house was hosting seventy-five kids a day eating food cooked on an open-flame gas stove out back. I had been calling in favors alongside my cohort Philip Peters, who is on the management team for Christian hip-hop recording artist TobyMac. Together, we harassed and bothered our music industry colleagues and friends until they helped sponsor the kids. And yet, even with seventy-five kids, there were still more standing outside the iron fence of the house every day. There was more need than we had funds. There was more to do.

I'M POSSIBLE

As a Visionary, Gerald moved at lightning pace, and not everyone could keep up. A Visionary can move so quickly and with such force that it strains relationships. Flashes of anger leave behind wounded folks. Gerald lost some friendships along the way, and many of them were a result of relational challenges intrinsic to Visionaries.

Conduit Church was still young, and Gerald and I were not yet aware of the need for the other six gifts to balance us. Thank God for His mercy because we certainly needed mulligans on some things. But if you were to ask any of the original fifteen of the thousand kids who are part of the program today, they would probably say they are grateful for an imperfect path toward building this ministry that has changed their lives.

Gerald saw what was possible and bulldozed his vision out of nothing. And what was possible? Fifteen years later,

Restoration Academy teaches 330 students daily. A sponsorship program pays for a thousand plus kids to go to schools in different villages throughout Haiti. A medical clinic offers healthcare to the community. More and more kids eat a hot meal every day. There's a home for young girls rescued out of high-risk situations. And a church of several hundred has replicated itself into three new churches.

In Haiti these days, there are leaders in the ministry who themselves were once children whose heads faced the ground. Those original fifteen kids are now high school graduates earning degrees from a university. Their eyes now meet your gaze. They're not looking down anymore; they're looking forward to a future made possible by the gift of a Visionary.

A principal named Rose, herself a teen when Gerald came back to Haiti, leads Restoration Academy. She went to university but did the unthinkable; she stayed in Haiti. She leads the school with confidence, joy, and vision. Those children see something in real life that Gerald saw through his gift: they see Rose. She's one of them. She did the impossible. These kids no longer see what is impossible. They see "I'm Possible."

That's today. Praise God! But Gerald Lafleur isn't done. The thing about a Visionary is there's no here-and-now; there's only future. Once the future becomes a reality, there's more vision. In a fallen world full of suffering, we need Visionaries to keep looking ahead and not settle for the here-and-now or the good enough.

Over the years, as I worked beside Gerald, there were many times I thought he would quit. It wasn't that he gave any indications of stopping; it's just that I would've quit if it were me. Over and again, I saw that we were out of options, out of time, out of money. But with Gerald at the helm, we were never out of vision.

Gerald wasn't blind to the facts; it's just that his vision was brighter. He moved forward as if success were guaranteed.

And that's what Gerald continues to do. He recently launched a Bible school to train young men and women to carry on the ministry. Land that will double the size of Restoration Academy is purchased. But Gerald Lafleur isn't finished. He's a Visionary; he's just getting started.

A VISIONARY'S MENTOR: THE APOSTLE PETER

Visionaries can look to the Apostle Peter as a mentor. He was the first to jump, the first to draw his sword, the first to speak up. He offended people early and often. He spoke out of turn and was perceived as a hot-tempered big mouth who continually challenged the status quo. He was Simon the fisherman, brother of Andrew, and one of the first to say *yes* to Jesus' invitation to follow Him.

Peter was the guy Jesus invited to walk on water with Him. Some say the other disciples missed out because they didn't make that leap; however, the truth is, Jesus didn't ask them to do that. He asked a Visionary to make that first step.

Why would Jesus ask Peter to walk on water and not the others? Maybe because Jesus knew that only a Visionary would take that risk. I think it's also because Jesus had a lesson for Peter and all Visionaries. As long as Peter kept his eyes on Jesus, he was doing the impossible. When Peter started looking at the circumstances around him, he began to sink. The Apostle Paul said in Romans 12 to "prophecy according to your faith." He was speaking of faith in Christ, not confidence in one's abilities. The lesson for Peter is a lesson for everyone, but especially for Visionaries: As you envision the future, make sure you're looking at Jesus."

Peter was the guy Jesus chose to lead the disciples after His resurrection. He needed someone to stand up and cast the vision for the church boldly. He needed someone who could stand firm in the face of blistering criticism, someone who could see clearly what no one else could yet see, someone who wouldn't back down in the face of opposition. Jesus needed a Visionary. He chose Peter.

Just a few weeks after Jesus' ascension, Peter stood in front of the same people who had called for Jesus' execution and boldly called them to repentance. Peter would first declare in the smackdab middle of Jerusalem that "this Jesus, whom you put to death," was the Son of God. That day, thousands became followers of Christ, and the church was born.

Was it because Peter had experienced a transformation? Yes. His Visionary gift had been honed, carved, sharpened, and strengthened in those three years with Jesus. His gift had been set free. The Holy Spirit was working in him, redeeming his weaknesses.

The same anger that propelled Peter to draw a sword in the Garden of Gethsemane and strike a Roman centurion focused on the vision of a new church being born in Jerusalem. Peter would face opposition, persecution, and ultimately death. But this Visionary saw God's glorious kingdom coming to earth—and he charged headfirst into the future. Peter put away his sword and opened his heart.

In the days after His ascension, Jesus told those to whom He had appeared to wait in an upper room for a sign that He was going to send. Ultimately, only 120 of hundreds of followers were present in that room, and Peter was there—front and center.

After the Holy Spirit enveloped that room, Peter stood first and challenged those gathered outside to see just what the commotion was all about. He told a crowd of thousands to repent. Peter then led the early church with purpose and urgency, demonstrating that when Visionaries are free and standing in their identity in Christ, they'll be strong, clear, and courageous.

RECOGNIZING A VISIONARY

The Visionary sees the future and can't understand why others can't. If you're a Visionary, you might not even realize you are vision casting. It's just instinct on your part. You're in Visionary mode—whether it's choosing a movie that's "going to be awesome!" or telling a coworker over whom you have no authority to do something.

Visionaries are self-confident, strong-willed, assertive straight talkers who are decisive. They can come across as overbearing and egocentric. It's not uncommon for others to perceive Visionaries as hot-tempered. However, when at their best, Visionaries use their strengths to improve others' lives. They are often heroic and inspiring. And Visionaries don't quit. They're competitive to the core. You also don't have to wonder what they're thinking, because they just said it.

For Visionaries, conflict is a synonym for connection. It's not uncommon for someone to say to a Visionary, "I don't want to fight about this," and the Visionary didn't know they were fighting. Though surprised by such acknowledgments, Visionaries are genuinely disappointed when others are hurt or harmed by something they said. Because of their confident assertions, it's easy to think that Visionaries don't feel remorse. But the truth is, they genuinely regret wounding others.

A Visionary firing on all cylinders will be unflinching, challenging the status quo and boldly declaring when something needs to change. Just because something has always been a certain way doesn't mean it should stay that way.

In day-to-day life, Visionaries are often entrepreneurs and leaders who launch something to solve a problem. They tend to land in some leadership level at companies or are successful in sales due to a sense of competitiveness. They use a high level of energy to accomplish goals head-on without procrastination.

It's essential for a Visionary follower of Jesus to love what Jesus loves and hate what He hates. A Visionary's confidence is a gift, but when it's not in submission to Christ, it puts one in the wrong posture—fighting for a cause not aligned with Jesus. Peter struggled with this. In the Book of Acts, Peter fought for the circumcision of all believers, which caused quite an uproar among the Gentile believers. Galatians 2:11-17 recalls that incident. The Apostle Paul said that he "opposed Peter very strongly," which is the best way to confront a Visionary. Conflict is connection.

There are times when what's important to Jesus will not be equally valued by men. In those situations, we need Visionaries on the front lines. They will lead the way and inspire confidence in the rest of us. But when Visionaries aim the gift at stuff that doesn't align with Jesus, they can lead others astray. As Peter taught us, we need Visionaries with eyes fixed on Jesus.

THE SEVEN WORKING TOGETHER

A Collaborator serves as the heart, hands, and feet that implement a Visionary's goals. (A Visionary without a Collaborator is just someone talking.) A Visionary can gather and lead but does so with extremely rough edges. Gut instincts working side by side with someone serving from the heart creates a perfect scenario.

A Discerner is good at reading the Visionary and connecting the dots for others. A big vision has many moving parts, and the Discerner's sweet spot is synthesizing seemingly disparate information so that everyone can grasp the image cast by a Visionary.

An Encourager helps infuse the emotional and spiritual fuel the rest of a team needs to keep going when the Visionary is plowing ahead. This fuel is vital because a Visionary can move forward with gusto—and assumes everyone else has the same energy level, which is rarely true.

An Imparter's ability to exude peace can create relational longevity and keep conflict from tearing apart a team and derailing the vision. Visionaries will always have a team around them, and where there is a group of people, there is conflict. An Imparter calms the water that a Visionary's gusto can churn up.

A Guardian is a scalpel touch for a Visionary's chainsaw approach. If you have the vision to feed children in Haiti, you need someone who can manage the funds, ensure food is evenly distributed, and cover the details. That's the beauty of a Guardian working in tandem with a Visionary.

A Responder notices and stops for those who are hurting so the Visionary can keep the vision moving. Visionaries are moving quickly toward the future, which means it's easy to miss the needs of those who are hurting. A Responder is a much-need salve that balances the force of a Visionary.

Are you a Visionary?

Chapter 6

The Collaborator

"Since God has so generously let us in on what He is doing, we are not about to throw up our hands and walk off the job."

– 2 Corinthians 4:1; MSG

AROUND THE HALLS of Conduit Church, Shannon Tyler is called the VP of TCB (Taking Care of Business). She is equal parts heart and grit, a force of nature who also happens to be my beautiful wife.

We first met in the early nineties when we attended the same Bible college in Tulsa, Oklahoma. At nineteen, Shannon loaded her giant Oldsmobile Cutlass and headed a thousand miles south from North Dakota. She did this solo with no cell phone or mapping software, and nobody riding shotgun. If you were to ask her at the time, it's not that she wasn't apprehensive about making that long haul by herself; she just did it anyway. That's what Shannon did then and continues to do. She sees what needs doing and does it. And that's the modus operandi of a service-hearted Collaborator.

Shannon's Oldsmobile presented a hilarious incongruity. Shannon is beautiful, petite, and sensitive—and yet she drove this gigantic, indestructible, brown piece of American-made machinery that was as plain as it was practical and could haul an army. It's the perfect picture of who Shannon is in real life. It's the picture of a Collaborator. On the exterior, Shannon is tough, resilient, practical—an unstoppable force. Inside, she's gentle, fragile, and all heart. Shannon doesn't take up or demand a lot of physical space but can drive people to reach a chosen destination. She is an external Oldsmobile Cutlass of indestructible practicality guided by a sensitive, beautiful soul.

Collaborators, like Shannon, are all business about getting stuff done. They come across as indestructible and levelheaded. When Shannon is in what she calls "the mode," you can join her and work alongside; she's got plenty of room for you. But don't get in her way, because she's moving forward with purpose and urgency.

When Conduit formed as a church, Shannon was in the starting blocks and ready to go. She was eager to serve, and she hit the ground running. We were a mobile church at that time, which meant setting up and tearing down every Sunday. Shannon brilliantly devised a plan that color-matched portable walls of children's classrooms with plastic tubs that contained items for the rooms. She was in constant motion from the moment the trailer door opened to the moment it closed.

While she loved organizing what once was the chaos of those early years, Shannon often felt frustrated and lonely. She had lots of great ideas and was ready to implement them; however, she rarely had a voice at the decision-making table.

Sadly, I was the main reason Shannon didn't have the opportunity to deliver her gift unfettered. I wanted to protect my wife from the firing squad of unspoken expectations. Being a pastor's wife is not a well-defined role, and people haul with them backpacks loaded with expectations from past experiences:

- A pastor's wife should play the piano and sing.
- She should lead the women's ministry.
- She should copastor.
- She should fulfill whatever role a favorite former pastor's wife filled.

I feared our church members would unload an avalanche of "you should" all over my wife. I knew the delicate Shannon who drove the Oldsmobile. I love her, and few things rile me more than someone bullying my wife. However, putting up boundaries to protect Shannon felt like a jail to her. I'm embarrassed that it took about four years to realize I was crushing Shannon and stealing her gift from our church family.

Shannon didn't need my permission to serve, but she certainly could've used my support. I had inadvertently blocked her purpose, shackled her from delivering the gift God gave her. And a lack of meaning for a Collaborator means thirst, and thirst means dying inside. We had a church family God had blessed us with that needed the gift of service God has entrusted to Shannon. By not inviting her into the journey, I robbed our church family of the gift of service God designed Shannon to deliver.

Slowly I awakened to reality. Regardless of the "you should" edicts others tried to impose on Shannon, God extended to her only one invitation: deliver the gift He had entrusted to her. Once I got out of Shannon's way, she blessed our church family in ways that would've never happened without her.

When God gave our church a 13,000-square-foot building and eleven acres of land, it didn't mean less work because we didn't have to set up and tear down week after week. Instead of working just one day a week, we now had responsibilities seven days a week.

We took possession of a building with all the charm of a government facility built in the seventies. Shannon had the talent to design and remake the entire building and the gifting to get it all done on a budget; however, her stubborn husband wasn't listening to her. In the first year of being in the facility, I had this idea that I didn't want to spend any money. Spending as much time as I did in Third-World nations, I fought against wasteful spending. We would use plastic chairs, and that was that. If our church friends in Uganda could sit on benches and a dirt floor, our church folks could sit on plastic chairs and carpet dated to the Crustacea Period.

However, during that first year in the building, I found myself dreading Sundays. I was glad when I was out of the country because it meant I didn't have to preach on Sundays.

Against all predictions, our church body hadn't grown much in its first year after moving into the building. Our attendance didn't shrink, but we had stopped growing. I loved the idea of being a church where we could challenge people in our affluent area to think as we think about the pain and suffering in the world. But we weren't going to get that chance because someone would visit one time, feel our facility's sterility, and never return.

The facility needed an overhaul. Architecture and design are spiritual. The subconscious feeling of "blah" people felt, including me, was due to its sterile personality when walking into our facility. I couldn't figure out how we would ever fund and redesign it, but I didn't have to. That was the gift Shannon delivered to our church.

Once she started, it was an Olympic-quality performance. Shannon recruited and collaborated with dozens of people to execute the vision. It was a flurry of hammers, saws, paintbrushes, and joy—an incredible thing to witness. The best part was watching how Shannon came alive during the process. It required long hours and navigating lots of complex relationships. But she loved it. Shannon, the Collaborator, was being who God created her to be.

The teams that worked on the renovation were folks who hadn't spent much time around one another but forged new friendships while working side-by-side. The church started to grow again. The people who visited the church began to stick around. One of the visitors remarked, "I love the interior of your church. When I walked in, it felt like the building hugged me." That's the perfect description of the work of a Collaborator. It's not just serving coffee; it's the love behind it.

The next project God gave Shannon was Place of Hope in Columbia, Tennessee, a 42,000-square-foot facility for recovering addicts. Conduit had a renovation vision that embraced "the least of these" but a limited budget for what seemed like an unlimited need. The building, a former nursing home, had sat vacant before Place of Hope moved in. It had the kind of tile you would've expected from an institution built in the sixties with a Stephen King movie's personality.

Shannon and I are active board members at Place of Hope (POH), so she knew the importance of giving its clients an atmosphere where they could recover in a peaceful and caring environment. She wanted the quality of the facility to match the excellence of the treatment they were getting. The budget we were working with required recruiting and collaborating with a small army of professionals and volunteers.

The POH Board of Advisors knew it was an impossible task with the amount of money we had available. We needed a miracle. We needed a Collaborator. The ministry couldn't ask someone to postpone their crisis. They couldn't shut down. The renovation had to include Shannon organizing rooms, moving clients for a few days at a time, and resetting rooms while managing contractors, choosing the design, dealing with all the unexpected obstacles that arise when renovating a decades-old facility.

Shannon brought together teams of volunteers working side by side. Her plan allowed them to experience the joy of sacrificing their time and resources for a more significant cause. It built community between the team members. And all those efforts now enable the clients of Place of Hope to experience freedom from drugs and alcohol in a beautiful, peaceful, and spiritual environment.

These days, if you're looking for Shannon, you have to be fast because she's moving with purpose and urgency and, generally speaking, she's moving beside someone she has recruited to help her. Not everyone can keep up, but those who do are part of the gift of the Collaborator. It's exhausting to watch her, and there are times I struggle to keep up. Shannon lives in a fulfilling way, and the world around her is better because she's finding the courage and opportunities to deliver her gift as a Collaborator.

A COLLABORATOR'S MENTOR: TABITHA

If you're looking for a Collaborator in the Bible, you'll find yourself in Tabitha's embrace. She was a Jesus follower who lived in Joppa. Acts 9:37-42 tells her story. She was someone who was "always doing good and helping the poor." Doing good. Helping. Those are the calling cards of a Collaborator.

Tabitha, an Aramaic word, means *gazelle*. There's hardly a more descriptive spirit animal for the Collaborator than the gazelle. They cover a lot of ground quickly and always travel in groups. If you've ever been to the plains of Africa, you know that gazelles work in teams to keep each other safe and protected.

We don't know the cause, but Tabitha died. Her death brought together in mutual mourning everyone she had been serving. Those she loved and served surrounded her, specifically widows who were poor and in need. Collaborators spend much of their time feeling invisible. They work so hard and fast that their efforts often go unappreciated—until they're not there anymore.

Acts 9:38-39 reveals that the widows Tabitha served heard that the Apostle Peter was in a town close by, so they sent word for him to come. When he arrived, they wept and showed Peter all of the clothes Tabitha had made for them while alive. "Look at everything she was doing for us! How can we survive without her?" As I said, Collaborators are easy to take for granted until they're gone.

Interestingly, when the apostles died, there is no mention of anyone asking for their return. But for Tabitha, the Collaborator, that's what happened. They were asking for God to raise her from the dead. She was so missed, loved, appreciated, and necessary that God allowed her to return to those who needed her.

It's impossible to know precisely why God chose to do this miracle. Still, I like to think Tabitha's return, at least in part, serves as a message for Collaborators: Even if you aren't recognized, and feel unseen, know that you are.

You won't get to attend your funeral, but if you're a Collaborator, know that the reaction to Tabitha's passing is the same response people will have when it's your turn to pass to the next life. The people who overlooked you and didn't fully appreciate you will wish you weren't gone.

Tabitha's life and death teach that the only eyes in the universe that matter are God's. Your Heavenly Father sees you. And even if no one else acknowledges you and your gift, God does. He cared enough to include Tabitha's name is in His Word. He cares enough to record your name in eternity.

RECOGNIZING A COLLABORATOR

Collaborators are everyone's dream friend. They love to give, and they place a high value on relationships. They are eager to volunteer their services if you need them. Collaborators are selfless; your needs come first. They remember everyone's birthday and anniversaries. They'll jump in to help organize your closet or garage. They'll take care of you when you're sick. They move quickly through tasks, accomplishing more before 10 a.m. than most can in an entire day. It's baked into their nature to give and put the needs of others above their own. They thrive as event planners, caregivers, doctors, homemakers, and any profession that helps others.

Collaborators lead from the heart. They are feelers who are sensitive. So it comes as a surprise that when under stress Collaborators can become assertive and respond with anger. Collaborators cry during movies and TV commercials. They feel before they think, and harsh words easily wound their hearts. Are Collaborators saints? Do they give for the sake of giving, and ask for nothing in return? Well, Collaborators are usually genuinely happy when they serve others. But they crave appreciation and their self-worth links to how helpful they are to someone.

Romans 12:7a instructs those who have the gift of collaboration to serve. There's an implied warning in that short statement. If you have the gift of serving, and you're using it to get something back, you're not serving; you're earning. And for a Collaborator, that's a path toward disappointment. Your sacrifice is for Christ, poured out for those who receive it. That's the calling.

Remember when Jesus visited the home of Mary and Martha? Mary sat at Jesus' feet to listen and honor him. Martha was busy doing the work. Collaborators struggle with recognizing when the doing can stop and the being can start. Martha needed Jesus to help her with that. He wasn't rebuking her; Jesus was setting Martha free.

THE SEVEN WORKING TOGETHER

A Visionary keeps the "why behind the what" in front of a task-focused Collaborator, attaching purpose to projects. Collaborators will sometimes be so focused on tasks; they forget there's a greater purpose for their efforts.

A Discerner helps an all-heart Collaborator think through decisions. The focused-on-facts Discerner enables the Collaborator to dial in on making a decision that may feel painful but is right based on the facts.

An Encourager keeps the energy and passion of a Collaborator ignited and serves as a wingman to encourage coworkers when the fast-moving Collaborator doesn't stop long enough to do it.

An Imparter has the knack for soothing frayed feelings and brings peace to a Collaborator, whose tasks usually link with some funding level. A Collaborator may come behind someone who has done a job and spruce it up a bit, which can feel demotivating and discouraging to the person who has done the task. The Collaborator means no harm, and an Imparter can soothe an unintended sting.

A Guardian thinks in pennies; Collaborators think in dollars. The two are a complimentary gift set. A Guardian ensures a Collaborator stays on budget, allowing the Collaborator to focus on the project. Collaborators lead with *yes*; Guardians lead with *no*. It's a tension that brings strength when they meet in the middle.

A Responder's kindness mode is the reminder for the serving Collaborator that it's okay to sit still for a while and be with someone. A Responder is in tune with the needs of others, the Mary balance for a Collaborator Martha.

Are you a Collaborator?

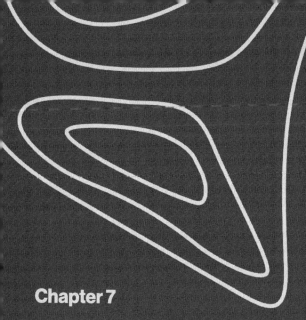

Chapter 7

The
Discerner

"If it is teaching, then teach."
– Romans 12:7; NIV

The Power of the Seven

"CURIOSITY KILLED THE CAT, but satisfaction brought him back."[3] If there's a better synopsis of Discerners, I don't know what it is. Rabid curiosity fuels their lives. It also gets them in trouble for asking too many questions or getting so engrossed in a topic that they ignore their loved ones.

I speak with authority here. I'm a Discerner. While growing up, there wasn't a boombox, alarm clock, or radio I wouldn't dismantle and reassemble to understand how it worked. Every single electrical outlet in my room had black marks around the edges from where I had plugged something in that shorted out in a terrifying and exhilarating display of sparks. It's no exaggeration to say it's a miracle I didn't burn the place down. The times I almost electrocuted myself number in the dozens.

It didn't stop with electronics. As a twelve-year-old, I stayed up late with a flashlight under my blanket reading the Bible. Not the Old Testament "Jonah and the whale story," but the Revelation "seven-headed beasts and the harlot riding it" story. Newspapers, periodicals, and the launch of CNN Headline News were a part of my life. I was a weird kid.

Fast forward twenty years. It was only a matter of time before church turned out to be the next boombox I was taking apart and trying to reassemble. I was deep-diving into the Bible, dismantling it in an attempt to understand why and how.

While I was trying to dismantle the Bible, God was dismantling me. He was rewiring my circuitry, connecting my head and heart. Sparks were flying inside of me. I wondered, *On previous passes through the Bible, how could I have missed so many commands about caring for orphans and widows? How did I not see the Scriptures permeated with warnings for rich people and the verses wired with encouragement for the poor and powerless?* The return of Jesus that I so obsessed about in the Book of Revelation was a promise of restoring the earth to the way it was in Eden. Jesus' invitation to "care for the least of these" was an invitation to build little outposts of His kingdom. Whispers of Eden. Glimpses of glory. It dawned on me that the question was not where is God in the midst of suffering in the world? The question was where is the church?

Dismantling isn't just deconstruction for the sake of deconstruction. That's destruction. The Discerner in me didn't want just to take the Bible apart; I wanted to put it back together again. That meant stepping away from the church that my wife and I attended in the Nashville area. I was a youth director at the time, and my dismantling mindset left black marks on the outlets from the sparks that flew. I wasn't trying to hurt anyone, including myself. But curiosity had me going.

I started by asking the two-word question that's wired into the DNA of every Discerner: *what if? What if I invited some friends to come together and study the Bible with me? What if we could be a conduit of resources from people who had plenty to those who had the greatest need?* It was a spiritual rewiring akin to *what if we took this wire from here and plugged it there?*

That's how Shannon and I, along with a gathering of others, connected with our group's name: Conduit, a channel for conveying something from here to there. Any correlation to a conduit being used to transfer electrical wiring was 100 percent lost on me. Who says God doesn't have a sense of humor?

We weren't a church; we were more like a Bible study group that refused to sit. We didn't take an offering; we just opened a channel. That isn't just semantics. In the early days, it wasn't much. A few hundred dollars here, a couple thousand there. But we were feeding and providing education for children trapped in extreme poverty in Haiti and helping homeless addicts in Middle Tennessee.

I thought that calling what we were doing a church would contaminate it. I was insistent that it was not a church. Shannon and I had landed at another church in the Nashville area, and were really enjoying it, and experiencing a time of healing. Confusing, I know, but I mean it when I say we weren't trying to do something correctly that everyone else was doing wrong. Jamie George, the pastor of that church, modeled humble servant leadership for me. If he was insecure that there was a guy who may have been pastoring a church inside his church, he never let it show.

Truth be told, Jamie helped open my eyes that the Conduit Bible study I was leading was indeed a church, and I was the pastor. The first time I floated by Shannon the idea of me being a pastor, I led with, "Do you know what Jamie said? He said that Conduit is a church, and I am a pastor." She laughed in the kind of way you laugh when you see a YouTube video of someone falling. She replied, "Darren, you don't even like people. How could you pastor a church?"

I had met and interacted with hundreds of pastors in my life. The successful ones all had one thing in common: they were Encouragers or Visionaries. I wasn't giving Pastor Jamie a humble, "Aw-shucks" response to his pronouncement that I was a pastor; I was looking at myself on paper, knowing that wasn't me. (Another quality of a Discerner is the ability to divorce from feelings and look at the facts.) But Jamie is an Encourager. He was giving me the courage to do what Discerners don't easily do: admit I was wrong.

If God wanted to build another large church with a centralized power structure and a dynamic communicator, then I wasn't the guy by a long shot. But if He wanted to create a scrappy, agile church that held on loosely to control, then I could plug into that. The God who wired me to love conduits showed me that someone like me could be a pastor (Ephesians 4) and lead it as a wired-for-change Discerner (Romans 12:7).

So, on Easter Sunday of 2010, Conduit Church was born. I'm still not sure it's accurate to say we started the church that day. It felt more like a moment when I had assembled the pieces of multiple churches (stereos). There was the suspenseful moment of plugging it into the outlet for the first time. Was it going to spew sparks and make a loud noise? Or would we experience that "Whew!" feeling when the little lights flickered on, and Aerosmith's sweet sound flowed out?

On that Easter Sunday, I had plugged in a mismatched pile of parts—and the sweet sound of Jesus was all around. It worked. No one was more surprised than this guy.

We had around 180 people join us on that first Sunday. In the following months, upwards of half-a-million dollars in cash and supplies flowed through Conduit to Haiti's earthquake victims. We were also sending teams to bring disaster relief to tornado and hurricane victims. And in between it all, we got together on Sunday mornings to worship and inspire each other to do good.

One of the questions I had asked was, "Why do we have to gather? Why can't someone be a Christian and not be part of a local church?" The answer is right there in plain letters in the New Testament. Remember that verse about "forsake not the assembling of yourselves together?" (Hebrews 10:25). It tells us why in that same sentence: "When you come together, inspire one another to good deeds." At Conduit, we figured out that as important as a good children's ministry and a worship band are, it's equally important to have a steady energy flow inspiring our church family to change the world.

In the Book of Acts, the Greek word *dunamos* (explosive power) describes the Holy Spirit's energy. Electricity was years from discovery, but the idea described power flowing from God through individuals. Turns out, God thought about this stuff long before anyone else did.

I do teach the Word on Sundays. The Word of God is active, alive, and powerful at Conduit. My teaching gift as a Discerner is integral to that. If you were to visit on a Sunday, you might not think we are any different than any other church. But under the hood, we're wired differently. Not better, just different.

The Discerner gift has made room for a church like ours in Franklin, Tennessee, with a church family of around 800 hundred people, but an impact that far outpaces our imprint. It is the conduit for millions of dollars that have helped the poor and powerless in the United States and worldwide. God made this possible because He wired me not to let it rest; I had to ask, "What if?"

The Conduit Church path hasn't been easy. As a Discerner, I lead from my head, not my heart. Remember those black marks around the outlets in my childhood bedroom? I've ignited a few sparks around Conduit because I've had to learn that just because I think something is fascinating, that doesn't mean it is. Our mission pastor, David Christopher, a Responder (see Chapter 11), once said that following me is like following a bottle rocket. It wasn't a compliment, but it's true.

As a Discerner, I'm a "Hard Hat" area at times, which has made my "let's think about church differently" obsession a long and sometimes lonely journey, not only for myself but for those I love. My wife knows what I think about almost everything, but she doesn't know how I feel about nearly anything unless she drags it out of me. As humans, God created us for connection. Information might connect dots for someone wired like me, but it doesn't link hearts, so I thank God for those with the other six gifts who link with mine to make Conduit a success.

A DISCERNER'S MENTOR: APOLLOS

When we search the Bible for a Discerner, Apollos flickers to life. He was an essential leader in the early church. We don't know much about his backstory, or where he ended up.

We do know he was an integral player in the new church, born in Greece. Acts 18 reveals Apollos was a learner, an accurate teacher, and someone wired to refute falsehoods with truth. All of these are traits of a Discerner.

> *"Now a certain Jew named Apollos, born at Alexandria, an eloquent man and mighty in the Scriptures, came to Ephesus. This man had been instructed in the way of the Lord; and being fervent in spirit, he spoke and taught accurately the things of the Lord, though he knew only the baptism of John. So he began to speak boldly in the synagogue. When Aquila and Priscilla heard him, they took him aside and explained to him the way of God more accurately. And when he desired to cross to Achaia, the brethren wrote, exhorting the disciples to receive him; and when he arrived, he greatly helped those who had believed through grace; for he vigorously refuted the Jews publicly, showing from the Scriptures that Jesus is the Christ." (Acts 18:24-28)*

"Apollos from Alexandra," sounds intelligent, doesn't he? And it's a logical deduction since his hometown housed the vast Library of Alexandria. The Scriptures describe Apollos as "eloquent," and "competent." As a Discerner of that era, Apollos wisely chose to be stationed near the library. It would've been the Google of its day—an endless supply of knowledge, nirvana for a Discerner.

Apollos spoke accurately about the things of God, but he knew only about the baptism of John. He needed more knowledge—likely craved it. When someone explained the way of Jesus to Apollos "more accurately," he accepted and applied it. And then, in full Discerner mode, he immediately began sharing the truth he had learned. In Acts 18:28, we discover that he "vigorously" refuted the Jews, "showing from the Scriptures that Jesus is the Christ."

Using his discernment gift, Apollos realized that John's baptism was not a bad thing, but it was incomplete. God was doing something new: salvation through Christ alone. Apollos saw the truth, adapted to it, and then shared the truth with others. That's the gift of the Discerner.

Later, Paul would describe the ministry of Apollos as "watering" (1 Corinthians 3:6). The gift of the Discerner is watering the seeds God plants in others at salvation. When someone comes to faith in Christ, a Discerner helps bring clarity to those who believe in the message of grace. If you're going to grow a seed, you'll need to water often, and a Discerner is a hose filled with the water of the Word, a conduit for truth.

RECOGNIZING A DISCERNER
Discerners are easy to spot. At a party, they're in the corner observing what's going on. They're reading at a coffee shop, and if they're wearing earbuds, they're listening to a podcast. At home, they're watching the Discovery Channel. Sometimes, they read a book while watching the Discovery Channel. The watchlist on a Discerner's Netflix account is full of documentaries and films about real-life events. Their capacity to absorb knowledge is somewhat mind-blowing, or mind-numbing, depending on how you look at it.

The Bible is a common focus for Christian Discerners. They also tend to specialize in specific disciplines. For instance, several Discerners I know are talented chefs, which makes sense because they thrive on discerning how separate things come together to create something great. A Discerner will often focus on a specific area or field and work to master it, concentrating on developing complex ideas.

Discerners thrive in taking seemingly disparate threads of information and synthesizing them. At their best, they are pioneers, often ahead of their time. They're able to see the world in entirely new ways.

The power of a Discerner is the ability to observe facts and situations and discern what is true. Although it can be confused with a desire to be right, truth is a Discerner's motivation. (Someone committed to being right isn't necessarily considering the facts as much as fighting for the feeling of being right. Being wrong is just too scary.)

A Discerner's quest is for information capable of creating meaning and purpose. The Discerner also seeks truth. Whether regarding church doctrine or judging a dispute between family members, Discerners are neutral because they lead with facts, not feelings.

Discerners are problem solvers with the ability to look at complex situations and identify possibilities. Because they are not overly emotional, Discerners are good at looking at all sides and can make decisions without bias. That's why they make great teachers, judges, and counselors. They shun drama and focus on the facts. By God's design, a Discerner asks questions to seek the truth. Without an emotional attachment to ideas, it's easier to move toward truth.

Discerners are alert, observant, insightful, and relentlessly curious. However, they can become preoccupied with their thoughts and imaginary constructs. They're a bit of a mystery because, on the one hand, they can become detached, yet on the other, they can be high-strung and intense.

Discerners are also adept at seeing something that already exists and how it could be different or better. They're skilled at leading an organization where change needs to happen. Discerners are natural connectors. They genuinely enjoy connecting people, which makes them good in situations where multiple things and individuals must work together for a common goal.

Fair warning: the mind of a Discerner is always running. Always. A Discerner's ability to look at all sides of an issue, with no felt need to land on something, can frustrate others. Also, Discerners can hesitate on decisions because they don't think they have all of the information. Sometimes this is true, but there are times when Discerners have to look at the facts and make a decision, even though they have a hard time knowing when that time has come.

Because of their ability to detach, Discerners tend to keep moving on to new ideas. As a Discerner who leads people, I've learned the hard way that this propensity can propel exhaustion. When others feel like they understand a mission, I develop a brand new one without warning.

Like most Discerners, I confess my desire to have all the information is a quest to feel safe in this world. Those around me can misinterpret this as intellectual arrogance. We Discerners tend to start a lot of sentences with two words: "I know." And if we don't find a topic interesting, we subconsciously check out. We don't leave physically, but it's not because we don't want to.

The tendency toward detachment can slide into isolation. Discerners like me need to fuse with those who bring the other six gifts' energy. And we work best together, like well-crafted transistors, when we recognize and follow who God wired us to be. In her book *Braving the Wilderness*, Brené Brown puts it this way: "True belonging doesn't require you to change who you are; it requires you to be who you are."[4]

THE SEVEN WORKING TOGETHER

A Visionary provides clarity for a study-all-the-options Discerner, which is a calming kindness and helps determine a clear future amidst all the options. Visionaries speak in matter-of-fact terms, which Discerners love.

A Collaborator instinctively looks at the colorful Legos,® a Discerner dumps out and knows what needs to get done and how to do it so the Discerner can move on to other things. Without a Collaborator, a Discerner will tend toward procrastination.

Encouragers help Discerners break out of analysis paralysis, infusing them with courage to take action. Discerners graze on information, but information doesn't inspire. Having an Encourager nearby helps to motivate others to enthusiastically apply information a Discerner has gleaned.

An Imparter, who instinctively knows how others feel about some-thing, is vital to healthy communication. Since a mind-focused Discerner pays little attention to feelings, working alongside an Imparter connects the mind of a fact-driven Discerner to the affects on people involved.

A Guardian ensures that things don't fall through the cracks, which keeps a Discerner out of hot water. Discerners are starters; Guardians are finishers who help protect the ideas of a Discerner. Guardians can help a Discerner look at all the information, and clarify it.

A Responder brings the heart and passion into the ideas of a Discerner, who's all head. The poet Maya Angelo often quoted author Carl W. Buechner, who said, "People won't remember what you said; they'll remember how you made them feel."[5] Discerners need Responders to remind them of that truth.

Are you a Discerner?

Chapter 8

The Encourager

"If it is to encourage, then give encouragement."

– Romans 12:8; NIV

I N AUGUST OF 2017, John Bisagno and his beautiful wife of sixty-three years, Uldine, were fighting for her life. Brain cancer was the unrelenting adversary, and a hospice nurse had recently made the first home visit.

While cancer was bearing down inside their house, Hurricane Harvey was bearing down from the outside. In just hours, the full-throttle hurricane shoved a muddy river into the Bisagno's neighborhood of thirty years. Downed trees and other debris churned in the torrent. Fading daylight and rising dark water trapped John and Uldine in their home.

By nature, John was walking joy. He was affectionately known as "Big John" because of his size, but it was a perfect description of who John was. His personality filled up a room, and his joy filled your soul. Even at 82, he was like a kid in a candy store, full of life and adventure. But Hurricane Harvey and Uldine's illness threatened to knock down the candy store.

That's when the "Cajun Navy" showed up in a bass boat. An informal band of Louisiana heroes floated up to the Bisagno home and carried Uldine on a homemade stretcher. They took her and the joyful love of her life to the safety of a friend's house on higher ground. Seventeen days later, Uldine was gone, as was their home and most of their possessions.

Cancer took Uldine; the flood took the rest. Remarkably, John didn't waver. His attitude was resilient. He told friends, "I've preached it as long as I've been preaching that Jesus is enough. Now, I've experienced it for myself. I've lost everything, and it's true. Jesus is still enough." If like me, you think *I could never do that*, it's probably because you're not an Encourager, who has a supernatural ability to hit life head-on with joy and resilience.

THE MAN BEHIND THE JOY

John became the pastor of First Baptist Church of Houston in the early seventies. At the time he took on the pastorate, it was a historic church that boasted 200 members near the downtown area. It was by no means a plush gig. The flight to the suburbs had begun, leaving John to fight an uphill battle of leading a church founded in the late 1800s only to find itself floundering in the 1900s.

By the time John retired some thirty years later, the church had grown to 22,000 members with an impact worldwide. Under John's leadership, this historic church experienced unprecedented growth even when the nation and Houston experienced downturns. The infamous oil bust of the 1980s was wiping out the financial standing of Houston's elite. The country was reeling from the Nixon impeachment crisis, the hostages in Iran, and economic uncertainty. But as an Encourager, John inspired those around him to overcome the odds and change the world. Encouragers like John don't have an ounce of quit in them.

John saw the world as full of possibilities. His optimism was contagious. It's an oversimplification to say he was an extrovert. He wasn't less than that, but he was so much more. He inspired a congregation to build what would become an expansive campus that changed the world around it.

John's optimism made him a trendsetter. He looked to other churches in the Houston area that were struggling and reached out to help them transform into thriving, impactful churches like FBC Houston. It's something done by many megachurches these days, but back then, it was unprecedented. When many pastors were worried that other churches were competition, John couldn't help himself. He saw them as friends and didn't want them to miss out on the incredible things God wanted to do. Dozens of churches regained life by being in the glow of John Bisagno the Encourager.

Over the decades, hundreds of men and women would find the courage to answer a call into fulltime ministry due to John Bisagno's influence and encouragement. I don't know the exact numbers, but the percentage of young men and women who found the courage to pursue vocational ministry is in the hundreds, not dozens.

Well-known Bible teacher Beth Moore is one of those individuals. She recounts the story of John summoning her to meet with him in his office. Beth hadn't yet become the famous Bible teacher. She was just a young woman with a calling who happened to be lucky enough to be an FBC Houston member.

She sat there in the open-door office with John's administrative assistant just outside. He had called Beth there to invite her to speak at the church. If you've been around the Southern Baptist denomination, you know that wasn't done in those days. A female Bible teacher remains controversial in many circles even today, never mind Jesus inviting two women to be the first preachers of the gospel after His resurrection.

Beth's immediate response was, "But John, I'm a woman."

John paused for a moment and shouted out to his assistant, "Carol, let me ask you something."

His secretary shouted back, "Yes, how can I help?"

Wide-eyed, with a mischievous grin, John replied, "Carol, did you know Beth is a woman?"

And then he laughed that big John Bisagno laugh. And the rest, as they say, is history! Beth accepted the invitation and counts John among the mentors who gave her the courage to follow God's calling on her life.[6] That's what John did for Beth Moore and many others. He inspired them, infused them with courage, and encouraged each to believe in what God could do through them.

As an accomplished musician, the trumpet was John's specialty. In his early days, he traversed the country as a trumpeting evangelist. Posters from that era showed the unmistakable joy of Big John while holding his trumpet, which is such an appropriate instrument for an Encourager. Historically, a trumpet signaled the charge into battle. The sound of a trumpet will one day mark the return of Christ himself. It's the perfect instrument-picture of an Encourager.

As a pastor, John played a new role—that of a conductor. If you've ever watched a symphony, you'll notice a conductor makes beautiful music without personally playing a note. The conductor's job is simple: awaken a group of musicians to the possibilities of what can happen if they work together. That was John Bisagno in a nutshell. That's the gift of the Encourager.

In November 2017, a few weeks after saying goodbye to his wife, possessions, and lifelong home, John moved to Nashville to live with his son, Tim, an elder at Conduit and one of my favorite friends. John became a part of the church I pastor.

Age and time had slowed Big John's body but not his Encourager spirit. He was in church every Sunday morning. He wasn't supposed to drive, but he bought a car to be on time and "make sure I get a good seat." John could've coasted. The guy had been in church his entire life, and after losing everything, nobody would've blamed him for sitting it out for a bit. But that never even occurred to him. Quit? Who does that? Not Big John. And not anyone in his gravitational pull.

John would tell people that he loved me, his new pastor. A man who had forgotten more about the Bible than I've ever known called me his pastor. Talk about encouraging!

As walking became increasingly difficult, John would show up with his walker and park it outside the office door and wait for me after service. He would tell me things like, "Darren, that was the best sermon I've ever heard," or, "You better hold on, buddy, because this church is going places!"

Let's be candid here. John had heard sermons from some of the greatest orators of our generation. He was one of them.

Factually speaking, I could whiteboard the reasons why mine wasn't the best sermon he'd ever heard. But in those moments, John wasn't speaking to my head; he was speaking to my heart. And in those moments, I believed him. He wasn't disingenuous. I think, at that moment, he thought it was the best sermon he'd ever heard. He lived in the moment, which is another mark of an Encourager.

Just by John showing up Sunday after Sunday, I was encouraged. Over the years, we've had the blessing of having experienced renowned pastors and Bible scholars visit Conduit. It's a mark of my weakness that I would still feel intimidated by men like that. But not John. Of anyone, I should've been most intimidated by him, but I wasn't. Not because I was so confident in myself, but because he was so confident in me.

In the summer of 2018, John preached his last sermon on this side of heaven at Conduit. Cancer was robbing him of clarity, but he was a tall glass of encouragement to everyone blessed enough to experience him in that sermon. His often-repeated words, "Boy, do I love you! Welcome to my heart!" still echo in the souls of many.

When John passed a few weeks later, his funeral was a parade of thousands of grateful people who loved John and whose lives were forever affected by him. Pastors, famous Bible teachers, lifelong friends, and beloved family members took turns at the microphone. And everyone who told stories about John used the same word: Encourager.

AN ENCOURAGER'S MENTOR: SILAS

Silas was a central figure in the early church. He's mentioned multiple times in the Book of Acts, as well as in Paul's letters. He was right there beside Paul during some of his most difficult times. When the Corinth church was hurting and confused, Paul sent Silas to give his gift of encouragement. "Jesus Christ, who was preached among you by...Silas...was not *yes* and *no*, but in him it has always been *yes*" (2 Corinthians 1:19; NIV). Encouragers lead with optimism. They lead with *yes*.

When you see Silas' name in Acts, it's always next to him encouraging or exhorting others. Acts 15 tells the story of discord in the churches over doctrinal issues. It sounds trivial just typing it, but the text reveals that this was critical during the church's early stages. The great movement Jesus started was in danger of imploding on the launchpad.

It took only a few verses to record this story, but it represented months. Feelings were hurt, creating wounds. While issues resolve, the hurt still stings. Through hard work, members with the seven gifts came together to resolve the issue.

So, Silas went to encourage the church. Paul sent him out with Judas (not that Judas). I'm reasonably confident Paul chose Silas for this role because he knew, at that time, those in the early church didn't need the gifts of a Discerner or a Visionary. Inserting an Encourager into a church conflict injects life and joy. Encouragers can bring levity to an intense moment. They take the situation seriously but not themselves. Acts 15:32 reveals that Silas said much to encourage and strengthen the believers. The words of Silas refreshed and bolstered others. The early church not only survived, but it also thrived. What could have been the first recorded church split ended not with the church breaking apart but coming together more robust.

But Paul still had a journey in front of him, and people were waiting on the ministry. It was going to be long days and longer nights. He couldn't do it alone. Whom did Paul choose to go along with him on his missionary journey? He chose Silas and hit the road, commended by the believers to the grace of the Lord. The two men, a Visionary and an Encourager, went throughout Syria and Cilicia, strengthening the churches.

During that journey (Acts 16), Paul and Silas were attacked, beaten, and imprisoned. There is the infamous moment when Paul and Silas were singing songs at midnight while locked in shackles inside a prison cell. *Who does that?* An Encourager, that's who. Taking an Encourager like Silas with him was what Paul needed in moments of uncertainty.

We know the rest of the story. An earthquake hit; the jail cell opened, and the jailer became a Christ-follower. After all of that, Paul and Silas went to their friends' homes and "encouraged them" (Acts 16:40).

As someone who has done a great deal of traveling around the world by myself, I know the value of having a travel partner. During those days when I've had Encouragers with me, I affirm the value in that gift. They make the trip fun and exciting. They're always up for an adventure. Of course, Paul chose Silas!

RECOGNIZING AN ENCOURAGER

The gift of encouragement isn't just a gift that makes others feel better; it's a gift that fuels others with the courage to be who God created them to be to do what He created them to do. They don't just give encouragement, they are courage. Encouragers don't just make you feel good about yourself; they make you feel glad about your calling. It's way more complicated than being cheerleaders. Encouragers miraculously inspire others. They "In" courage! Big John's often repeated encouragement, "Be true!" speaks to that.

The church needs Encouragers to get us through the hard times and so that we won't miss the good times. While those with the other six gifts might get so busy, they miss the moment; Encouragers won't let that happen. John's son Tim is Encourager 2.0 in my life. When I'm around Tim, I don't know what will happen, but I know it's going to be awesome. I always leave that guy feeling better about life.

Encouragers are adventurous and future oriented. They are eternally optimistic, extroverted, and love being around people. They are confident something better is just around the corner. Typically, they are quick thinkers, energetic, creative, open-minded, and often hilarious. My friends that have this gift are a blast on a road trip. It's very common for Encouragers to be successful. Their own lives serve as inspiration.

Encouragers can struggle with an unawareness of time, which makes them consistently late. To them, it's not that they're inattentive; it's that others are paying too much attention. An Encourager's general sense of optimism perceives more is doable in the time available than reality dictates.

It's not uncommon for Encouragers to avoid their pain and fears. They are warriors of encouragement, and there's a proclivity toward not wanting to face personal issues. It's not as simple as ignoring those; it's more like not being aware of them. And without dealing with them, people with this gift lean toward loneliness.

Interestingly enough, the Encouragers I know don't tend to see the value in their gift, which is quite ironic since those around them understand it well.

Focus can be a challenge for Encouragers. They are often fantastic at so many things and so quickly bored that it's not uncommon to have a wide array of projects going on at any given time. Maybe that's why Paul instructed Encouragers to "give that gift" as a reminder that focus will be a challenge!

An Encourager might be late to the party, but the party doesn't start until an Encourager shows up. That's why we need Encouragers to keep showing up. They possess the gift that keeps giving. Encouragers thrive in roles that allow them to inspire, such as personal trainers and children's ministry.

THE SEVEN WORKING TOGETHER

A Visionary channels the full-throttle Encourager to focus on the projects that can have maximum impact. Both are high-capacity gifts, but Visionaries can help Encouragers to confront hard situations and have the difficult conversations.

A Collaborator's heart steers the Encourager to embrace the contributions of those working alongside of them. Encouragers tend to move quickly but need Collaborators to rally the troops to complete tasks.

A Discerner helps an Encourager process information and synthesize the moving parts. These two gifts tend to work well together. Encouragers can rely on Discerners to think through all the facts and information to craft a quantifiable mission.

An Imparter helps the energetic Encourager recognize when people around them are genuinely tired or emotionally drained. The Imparter's sense of how others are feeling brings equanimity.

A Guardian enables an Encourager—who moves quickly—to stay on track. The Guardian also cleans up all the unfinished business the energy of an Encourager produces.

A Responder recognizes that Encouragers are not fans of sadness or pain. In a world where those things are a reality, a Responder helps an Encourager move through a season of hurt, instead of ignoring it. Responders also help Encouragers to see those around them who need to heal before encouragement can take.

Are you an Encourager?

Chapter 9

The Imparter

"If it is giving, give generously."

– Romans 12:8; NIV

The Power of the Seven

MY FRIEND NICK DE PARTEE was twenty-one when he started touring professionally with rock bands as a guitar tech. To put it differently, he was a caddie for guitar players. Nick is a kind, affable, peace-loving guy, the person whose call you always want to answer when you see his number pop up. Everybody loves him. He's a giver, not a taker, someone who has often given at the expense of having nothing for himself. Nick is a true-blue bona fide Imparter.

I first met Nick when he was the guitar tech for Kutless, a Christian rock, guitar-driven band I was managing. The group had two guitar players, which is the equivalent of a car with two gas pedals. It's not so much about going twice as fast as being twice as cool. Those boys had enough guitars and gear to stock the music section of a pawn shop.

Guitar tech is one of those jobs most people don't even know exists. It's not what little children dream of being when they grow up. The dream is to be the rock star, not the guitar nanny. It's a long day of heavy lifting, tuning, adjusting—and then you hand the flawless instrument to the guy on stage wearing the leather pants, and he gets to be the hero.

The guitar tech's job is 100 percent about giving to the guitar players so they can focus on the gig in front of them. The tech takes on all the stress and energy required to make sure an instrument is in perfect working order before it goes on stage. There is a fascinating amount of mental skill needed for a guitar to be ready to go. The performer has plenty of pressure to hit the right notes. But if you hit the right notes on an out-of-tune guitar or a guitar isn't correctly connected to the system, that doesn't matter. The gift isn't the guitar; it's the peace of mind that comes with knowing that the instrument is ready on the first note when in your hands.

Nick was every bit as talented as the guys to whom he was handing the guitars, but he never once jockeyed, postured, or commented about how he could do their jobs. Imparters are givers, not takers. Whatever chaos that comes with a major band tour, and it's plentiful, Nick was there in the background. He was a human thermostat who could quietly adjust the emotional temperature to a comfortable setting.

For a guitar tech, the lack of money only eclipses the lack of glory. It's not quite an internship, but only in the sense that you're not the one making the coffee run. Nick spent his days tuning, polishing, restringing, and loading gear. He did it without complaining. Humility is a noticeable trait in an Imparter.

"Growing up," Nick said, "I never wanted to be Batman; I wanted to be Robin. I didn't want to be the guy, but almost the guy."

When he reflects on that season of his life, Nick remembers it as an incredibly hard time, but not because of his work. He didn't mind that at all. The difficulty was being part of a band that was succeeding on stage but was inundated backstage by internal conflict.

Kutless had gold records, sold-out shows, number one radio singles—and the relentless travel schedule that goes along with them. It's a fascinating social experiment that we do on bands. We give them fame, fortune, and the expectation of always being awesome. When it's a Christian band, we pile on the expectations that they live exemplary lives and preach like experienced seminary graduates. We put them on the road away from their families and then handcuff them together in a shoebox on wheels twenty-four hours a day, 300 days a year. It's no wonder conflict reverberates in most bands.

As the guitar tech, Nick was right in the middle of the discord but still outside. There were lots of closed-door meetings after blow-up fights and the kind of bitter tension you can taste. As their manager, I found myself in the middle of many of those skirmishes. I need to let you know that these were and are fine young men. The conflict was everyday life on the road for almost every act I ever represented. I watched those guys grow from kids to fine young men, husbands, and fathers. I'm proud of every one of them.

What I remember is Nick being a great guy and so loved and yet ready to be done with the drama. It wasn't the workload or the fact that someone else always got the glory. And it wasn't just the conflict. Nick has the gift of imparting peace, but he couldn't deliver it where it was needed most in the band because he wasn't in the band. Handing those guys guitars but not his gift of peace wore Nick down. He didn't have any language for what he was feeling. None of us did. But the thing about feelings is that just because you can't name them doesn't mean they aren't there.

Nick would say he hates conflict, but what he means is he loves peace. His love of and desire for peace is one of the God-given gifts of an Imparter. It's not just that he's peaceful; he is. But get me when I say Nick is peace. By simply walking in the door, Nick produces calm in a storm. His peace mode allows him to see both sides of a conflict. He can intuit how people are feeling. He lays aside his preferences and feelings so that he can feel those of others. Nick had what the band needed most in a sea of discord, and it wasn't a drop-D tuning.

Eventually, one of the Kutless guitar players needed to come off the road permanently. His wife was pregnant, and their beautiful baby girl was having health challenges. As you might imagine, this was a scary time for everyone, a sea of uncertainty while the Kutless song "Sea of Faces" was rocketing up the charts. Nick was the perfect guy to fill in, but it goes to show how hard it was for peace-loving Nick when you know that this wasn't an automatic *yes* for him. More than being in the band, he needed to be invited into the circle.

Thankfully, Nick did take the stage with Kutless. The conflict didn't stop or slow down. Like ice cubes added to boiling water, the discord didn't cease, but there was a regulator. I firmly believe that Nick joining the band bought them several more years of touring and success. I'm not talking about his guitar skills, though they are superb. Nick's very presence kept emotions from boiling over. His peace flowed from his soul, calming others toward unity. His generosity, often given with personal sacrifice, served as a bridge between strained relationship gaps. That's a perfect picture of an Imparter.

These days, Nick uses his skills as a graphic artist to help fuel a technology start-up with some former touring musicians. He is married to a beautiful Guardian named Allison, and they are parents of three incredible sons. His ability to pour out his life continues to bring calm and steadiness to everyone around him, including me.

An Imparter's Mentor: Titus

Titus was a consistent traveling companion of the Apostle Paul. It's oddly fitting that a guy who takes up so much space in Scripture doesn't get his own storyline. You have to piece it together from the various mentions throughout the New Testament (of which there are many). There is a letter written to him but not one written by him. That's an Imparter—giving so much to others that his own life fades into the background of those served. If Paul was Batman, Titus was Robin.

Here's what we do know. Titus was of Greek background and well-educated. His name means honorable. (I can't think of a better word to describe every Imparter I know.) When you look at Titus' life, you see that he was a problem solver, an administrator, and a peacemaker—an Imparter's hallmarks.

Titus was in the background, but make no mistake, he was fully present and played a critical role in the early church's success. A new movement was born, churches planted, and lives saved. Whenever that happened, Satan wasn't far behind, trying to destroy from within what he was unable to destroy from without. Strife and warring factions are primary tools of the enemy. And the Imparter is one of God's best weapons against such devices.

When a famine in Jerusalem required financial support, Paul sent Titus to collect the funds. The church at Corinth had the financial means to help those in Jerusalem; however, they were such a hot mess of division and hurt, working with them required someone who had a gentle but firm touch. When Paul wrote his first letter to the Corinthians, he sent Timothy to deliver it. But the second time around, he sent Titus the Imparter. It was not an easy task. Titus' mission was to navigate the rough terrain left behind by Paul's previous words (1 Corinthians) and the repercussions of what the apostle referred to as his "painful visit." The people in the Corinth church were upset. Paul's Visionary gift spoke forcefully and truthfully. But his words left hurt feelings and angry people. Titus' job wasn't just to commiserate with them and perpetuate their feelings. His role was to bring peace, and that's a home-field advantage for an Imparter.

The stakes were super high. Not only was unity at risk in this early church, but there were fellow believers in Jerusalem who were under persecution and famine. They desperately needed financial help, and the church at Corinth was superbly capable of helping these oppressed saints. If the Corinth church had imploded, the consequences would have been far-reaching.

And how did it go? Titus knocked it out of the park. When Paul sent Titus back to the church at Corinth, he included a letter that told the Corinthians just how encouraged and happy he was:

"But God, who comforts the downcast, comforted us by the coming of Titus, and not only by his coming but also by the comfort you had given him. He told us about your longing for me, your deep sorrow, your ardent concern for me so that my joy was greater than ever." (2 Corinthians 7:6-7; NIV)

In this letter, Paul appealed for the generosity of the church to help the saints in Jerusalem. Who were they going to trust to carry this offering to Jerusalem? Titus. He had been willing to give up his life for them, and in doing so proved himself trustworthy for such an important role. Remember, they didn't deal with checks or credit cards. Titus would be carrying large sums of coins that would need to be delivered by someone who wasn't skimming a portion for self-gain. As an Imparter, generosity is natural. When you give your very life, money isn't something that motivates you; it's just another highway on which you impart peace.

RECOGNIZING AN IMPARTER

The Greek word the Apostle Paul used for giving, *metadídōmi*, means to "impart." To suggest that imparting is just about giving money is to misunderstand what it means to be an Imparter because it means so much more.

Imparters are peacemaking, charitable empaths. They can sense what everyone in the room is feeling. If there is a disturbance in the force, they perceive it immediately. Their reflex response is to impart peace and bring balance. Imparters don't just give of their time, treasure, and talents; they give themselves.

Imparters are optimistic, supportive, and bring people together. They focus on the bright side of life. I have found them to be that trusted, steady hand on the wheel. They want everything to go smoothly. They will tell you they hate conflict, but the reality is that they love peace. One challenge for Imparters is that they tend to minimize a problem to avoid creating upsetting situations. Ironically, Imparters can be one of the most stubborn of the seven gifts, but at their best, they are welcoming and able to heal conflicts and bring people together.

In 1 Thessalonians 2:8, we read, "So having great love toward you, we were willing to impart to you not only the gospel of God but also our own lives, because you were dear to us." This verse sums up the Imparter spirit.

For a team to function, it requires that members give into the broader vision, and Imparters excel in this. It makes them easy-going, amiable, and inclusive. Seeking harmony in a team environment is a super-power Imparters have on tap. Their generosity lies in giving themselves wholly to those around them. In doing so, they don't focus so much on how they feel as they can sense what others around them are feeling.

Paul challenged Imparters to give with simplicity (Romans 12:8). This guidance is a beautiful warning for an Imparter to have healthy boundaries and realistic expectations. Imparters give themselves. They give up their preferences, desires, and feelings to allow others to have theirs. They focus on other people's agendas and the external environment. They can do this for years, stuffing down their own needs and emotions, but eventually this leads to burnouts and blowups. Paul's warning was to stop that long before it happens.

It takes tremendous strength to live like this. And that's why Imparters must maintain a unique sense of equilibrium. They can fall into a "peace at any cost" hole. Avoiding conflict with others also can keep Imparters from being fully present in relationships. In a quest to give themselves wholly to others, they lose themselves in the process. In marriage, friendships, or the workplace, this depletion can lead to unspoken resentment. Avoiding conflict can also lead to a kind of inertia and sidetrack Imparters from God-given personal priorities.

Imparters are also at risk for numbing practices (food, drink, or entertainment) to avoid conflict, manage anger, and maintain a comfortable or harmonious self-image. That's why it is vital for Imparters to continually replenish their souls and remember the promise Jesus gave for giving is that when you give yourself, God will give back to you.

An Imparter gives so effortlessly it's hurtful when others don't recognize the sacrifice. If the giving goes unnoticed, others might perceive the Imparter as "fishing for a compliment or an atta boy." In reality, the Imparter is craving connection. Paul's directive to give with "simplicity" is an encouragement not to seek reciprocation. Just give, and trust that Jesus will give it back to you. And that's a core reminder for an Imparter. An Imparter's gift will frequently be unreciprocated by those receiving it. But even if no one else gives in return, an Imparter can know that the most important eyes in the universe, the One who breathed life into existence, receives it. And He reciprocates by imparting the peace that surpasses understanding.

THE SEVEN WORKING TOGETHER

A Visionary keeps an Imparter moving forward to break out of inertia. Imparters are fantastic at mediating other people's conflicts but often step back when it's their own. Visionaries have a way of forcing schisms into the open.

A Collaborator supplies motivation and can help an Imparter—who tends to be more passive—take direct action. When Imparters might "go it alone" because they don't want to impose on others by asking for help, Collaborators come alongside to rally the troops.

The Discerner brings logic and curiosity to the peaceful, easy-going Imparter. Discerners bring forward practical solutions and a buffet of knowledge. This track helps Imparters be more objective and rational when making decisions.

The Encourager brings creative new ideas to the surface, helping Imparters feel more confident in themselves and their ideas. Imparters hate the feeling of imposing on others, but in moments when help is needed, Encouragers are there to bring the courage needed to move forward.

The Guardian brings hard work and commitment to the table. Guardians help Imparters feel more comfortable sharing their opinions and ideas. Guardians also help Imparters with saying *no*. Imparters lead with *yes*, and a Guardian brings a sense of the reality of the restrictions of a twenty-four-hour day.

A Responder imbues creative thinking and emotional awareness to help an Imparter understand personal feelings. When Imparters are unsure of their own feelings, Responders are able to dig deep.

Are you an Imparter?

Chapter 10

The Guardian

"If it is to lead, do it diligently."
– Romans 12:8; NIV

The Power of the Seven

MARTIN THIEMAN WAS BORN in the Rust Belt. Dayton, Ohio—one of the cities hardest hit by economic recession and outsourcing—was his home. It was the perfect training ground for a Guardian. Empty factories and padlocked chain-link gates wrecked the landscape. Why? Because someone failed to anticipate looming dangers.

When Martin was a teenager, he played the role of Moses in one of those youth-group-type skits. His youth pastor called him Mo during rehearsals, and the nickname stuck. Maybe it was a coincidence, or perhaps God was confirming something about the way He had wired Martin Thieman from the get-go. You see, Moses killed an Egyptian who was abusing Israeli slaves. He's the one who pushed through the fear and stood up to Pharaoh. Moses was a Guardian for Israel, a shepherd. And that's Mo, the ever-watchful Guardian.

In his early twenties, Mo was a music industry artist manager. By that point, he was married, had two children, and owned a home. Long before most young men were even thinking about the future, Mo was planning for it and actively working in that direction. (When I was in my early twenties, I was actively not married and rented half of a duplex.)

During that season, I managed headline music tours and had the privilege of hosting some of Mo's clients. He had this uncanny ability to anticipate what could go wrong. Mo would continually ask, "what if this happens?" and "what will we do when?" If you've not been in the music industry, you might not know this, but the answer to most questions like that is, "Man, I don't know; we'll have to figure that out when we get to Wichita."

I immediately liked Mo when I met him. (That's not unusual; everyone likes Mo. He's consistent, loyal, steady, and hilarious.) He spoke like someone who had lived a lot of life. In reality, he was a young guy who had thought a lot about life and what might happen, so he prepared himself for it. He had lived life in his mind before living it on foot.

While this sounds so simple in writing, a real war was going on inside Mo. It's the conundrum most Guardians face: How do I meet the future's potential dangers without letting them consume me? It was almost as if an internal battle raged between Martin and Mo. Martin looked to the future filled with its uncertainty and could get paralyzed by the dangers. Mo would push past those fears and lead into the future, fully prepared for all the possibilities. It wasn't that Mo wasn't afraid; he did it anyway because he prepared. That's a Guardian.

During his decade in the music industry, Mo signed bands that would be quite successful. When Mo discovered those bands, no one had ever heard of them. What would possess a young group to sign a management contract with a twenty-something rookie? Because they felt safe with Mo. As a manager, he always had their backs. He was fiercely loyal when negotiating on their behalf. And while other managers would vent about their clients, I never heard Mo do that. He was pleasantly persistent and guarded their business and personal interests as if they were his own.

Mo's music career was full of the highest highs and the lowest lows—and he kept hitting the ceiling. He would get music artists up and running, working with them to achieve a solid track record of success, and then they would leave him to sign with a more prominent manager. They would say things like, "Mo, we need someone who can see the big picture" or the patently ridiculous verbiage, "Someone who can take us to the next level." It might be a coincidence, but those clients didn't manage to go up any levels after moving on from Mo.

I'm not just saying this because Mo is my friend. I don't say this because I want him to feel better if he reads this book.

I'm writing this because I know it's the truth. Those bands misconstrued Mo's ability to see the obstacles and potential dangers as someone unable to see the big picture. They viewed his ability to anticipate danger as an inability to navigate their careers. The irony is that his ability to see the risks ahead brought them the success they were enjoying. What they misperceived as lack of vision was crystal-clear foresight.

WE NEED MO

In 2014, Conduit Church began to see significant growth in both attendance and generosity. We needed someone who could protect the vision. We needed someone who could oversee the finances, corral the details, and anticipate the risks that we were facing in the future. We needed someone to scan the horizon for incoming threats. We needed someone who could imagine things that could go wrong. We needed someone to ponder possibilities. We needed a Guardian. We needed Mo.

I could've placed an ad on LinkedIn and pulled in dozens of qualified candidates with the required skillsets. We could've hired someone with proficiency in Excel and organizational skills. However, the church didn't just need an accountant; we needed a Guardian. We needed a Mo.

Mo and his wife and children were already part of our church family, but his gift was something that could protect Conduit. His gift opened that door. He came on board as an executive pastor and had to learn a set of skills and harvest new knowledge. What one can't learn is the Guardian gift. You either are, or you aren't. We didn't hire Mo for his skills; we hired him for his God-given gift. Mo's job description is thorough and broad, but his job responsibility is focused, honed, and simple: just be Mo.

Our church has grown exponentially in both attendance and generosity since Mo came on staff. I don't think that's a coincidence. Because of him, the exponential growth didn't derail us from our vision and mission. Because of Mo, our church family feels safe to give because we have checks and balances. They feel safe to bring their kids because we have protective measures in place. They feel safe to invite their friends because nothing is going to get nutty.

As the Guardian of Conduit, Mo protects our integrity and money, our vision and mission. In doing so, he has developed and executed systems, recruited and trained leaders, and made sure the propane tanks are full for the winter. His systems anticipate problems and solve them because that's who Mo is. Intuitively, he's perpetually running assessments and thinking about everything that can go wrong. Nothing surprises him because he has already considered that it could go wrong. That's the beauty of those gifted as Guardians. They're always on the look-out.

Did Mo bring his gift to Conduit? Or is Mo the gift to Conduit? The short answer is yes. I'm attaching a name to each of the seven God-given gifts because each gift is part of a person. The gift isn't a thing. The gift is me. The gift is you. And the gift is Mo. He was paid for and set free by Christ and given to Conduit by Christ Himself.

Oh, by the way, Mo is also an extremely talented graphic designer. His penchant for creativity has earned him a stable living. He continues to do much of the design work that sets Conduit apart in the world. But Mo's Guardian gift is what allows me to sleep at night. I know he's worried about what's coming, so I don't have to. There's a cost to this gift, and Mo knows it well. A Guardian's gift to others is a burden. It's because Mo doesn't sleep well that I can.

A GUARDIAN'S MENTOR: MOSES

Moses had the ideal job for a Guardian—protect the sheep. That one job takes on many facets. A successful shepherd has to anticipate the dangers that lie ahead and make preparations to mitigate—mapping out the grazing patterns based on what worked in the past, predicting where the water is going to be and where it's not.

From the estimated three million Jewish people at the time, God chose Moses to be His messenger and lead Israel's people out of captivity. God needed someone who could anticipate the dangers that lay ahead—and adapt.

How do we know Moses was a Guardian? Well, Exodus 2 gives us the first clue. We see his conversation with God at the burning bush. Moses told God all the reasons the gig wouldn't work. In essence, Moses was anticipating the dangers. Verse 11: "Who am I that I should go to Pharaoh?" Verse 13: "Suppose I do go (not committing to anything just yet, but hypothetically speaking). Who will I tell them sent me?"

Remember, God was speaking to Moses from a bush that was on fire. That in and of itself was pretty convincing. But Moses had more questions. In Exodus 3:1, he asked, "But what if they don't believe me?" With that, God told Moses to throw his wooden staff on the ground; it became a snake. A snake! Then God told Moses to pick up the snake—and it turned back into a wooden staff. God then gave Moses leprosy on his hand and healed it. Burning bush, miraculous snakes, leprosy, and what was Moses' response? Verse 10: "Pardon me, but I'm not very eloquent. I am slow of speech and tongue." With that, God reminded him that he had a fast-talking brother named Aaron, who would go with him.

God chose Moses precisely because of his gifting, not despite it. His response to Moses' question from verse two was, "What's in your hand?" It was a staff. "Moses, that thing you are gifted to do, to guard, that's what I'm asking you to do." God wasn't choosing Moses despite of who he was but because of who he was.

Moses told God all the reasons it wouldn't work. He had anticipated all of the dangers, which is why God chose him! It's not that God didn't know those things. It's helpful to remember that when God calls you to do something, He has already factored in who He created you to be. He's smart like that.

We also can learn from Moses the opportunity to grow a gift. At some point, Moses had to admit that he possessed all the necessary information and decided to obey God. As a Guardian, the ability to assess dangers is the gift. However, there's a point when a Guardian must look at the dangers and not see them as the reason to hold back but to charge forward because the risks are visible and manageable.

Recognizing a Guardian

The word translated into English as lead or rule derives from the Greek word *proïstēmi*. It means to preside or set over, but with the underlying motivation of guarding and protecting. When Paul wrote to Titus, he challenged him to "be careful to *maintain* good works." The word maintain in Paul's letter to Titus is the exact word the apostle used in Romans 12:8. Paul was saying, "Titus, make sure that the good things you are doing for widows, orphans, and those in need are done wisely and carefully." Titus needed to guard those ministries.

You now know that Titus was an Imparter. His gift of imparting peace required a Guardian nearby. The Guardian ensured that others did not take advantage of Titus. The Guardian guaranteed food was distributed to widows equitably and finances channeled correctly.

Guardians are orderly, organized, and detail-oriented. They are ethical with a strong sense of right and wrong. Guardians always strive to improve things while making sure processes are in place, and order is maintained.

Loyalty and honesty are things Guardians value. At their best, Guardians are wise and discerning, knowing the best actions to take in each moment. They have a passion for the truth, and they protect it. Guardians are rational with an intense sense of right and wrong. They are principled, fair-minded, have a sense of responsibility, and are dependable.

When firing on all cylinders, Guardians remain faithful to the people and communities around them. More than that, they build trust that propels a team or organization forward. In ministry, this means the ability to build confidence in ways that point people to Jesus. Because people know Guardians are on their side, building a team to pursue a mission is fun and faith-building.

Guardians influence in ways that build momentum for teammates and challenge them to consider new directions. This trait makes Guardians great team players and useful influencers. In relationships, they are dependable partners and loyal friends.

The biggest fear of a Guardian is detachment—being abandoned by others and remaining alone. It can make a Guardian's most significant strength—loyalty—show up as a weakness. It means that, sometimes, the commitments of dedication and protection are rooted in fear. This mindset can lead to anxiety and stress. In those moments, a Guardian might over-perform or over-commit to compensate for the fear.

For a Guardian, self-confidence comes from the affirmation of others. When that affirmation is absent or thin, the tendency is to struggle with self-doubt. When challenging events unfold, a Guardian can sometimes develop overwhelming and debilitating anxiety from the illusion of constant danger.

Guardians are mentally acute, yet highly skeptical. They seek security and group approval for their actions. They are often acutely aware of their shortcomings, and their self-esteem may fluctuate. When Guardians sense a disconnect between themselves and their group, they can become noticeably agitated and nervous. To prevent disappointment, Guardians mentally prepare themselves with worst-case scenarios before carrying out a task. The negative side effect is the perception that the Guardian can't do the job.

Guardians can tend to over-analyze information as it comes in. They have to watch for this in their jobs, marriages, and parenting. They need to challenge themselves to say *yes* more than *no*.

The Apostle Paul encouraged Guardians toward diligence—to reframe motivation from fear to an earnest and persistent action. For the Guardian, perseverance is the optimum weapon against panic and cycles of worry.

THE SEVEN WORKING TOGETHER
A Visionary helps a Guardian move to action before he or she feels ready. When a Guardian can see all that can go wrong, a Visionary motivates with what will go right.

A Collaborator comes alongside a Guardian and breaks through roadblocks to get a project moving. Most times, while the Guardian is still assessing a situation, the Collaborator moves forward to execute the plan.

A Discerner helps a Guardian sort through threats to sift the credible from the imaginary and enables a Guardian to break the paralysis logjam.

An Encourager brings a Guardian much-needed affirmation about personal achievements and group dynamics. An Encourager breathes a sense of life and joy that bolsters a Guardian.

An Imparter brings the gift of peace to the heart of an anxious Guardian. The Imparter senses when something isn't right and moves to bring equanimity into a Guardian's life. In a sense, an Imparter guards the Guardian.

A Responder brings heart to the head of a Guardian. Threat assessment is primarily a head exercise. A Responder's nature brings mercy to those around a strict-minded Guardian.

Are you a Guardian?

Chapter 11

The Responder

"If it is to show mercy, do it cheerfully."

– Romans 12:8; NIV

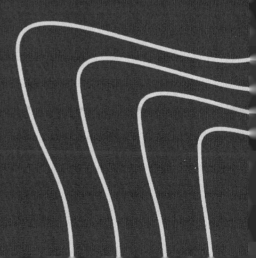

WHEN THE STUFF HITS THE FAN, David Christopher is the guy you want beside you. He's not going anywhere. He's there for the duration. Romans 12 calls this the gift of mercy. The closest English word we have to the Greek word used in that passage is "succor," which means to *give aid*. As English words go, that one kind of sucketh.

So, why did I give those with the gift of mercy the title Responder? Because the original Greek word speaks of someone not just giving aid but giving aid to those during their time of need. Responders have this sixth sense to see the afflicted that the rest of us miss. They don't just walk by; they respond. That's the gift of David Christopher.

David lives his life from his heart. He's passionate and courageous. With cool Bono-hair, double-hoop earrings, and a distinct sense of style, David stands out in a crowd. And if a crisis should hit a group, they're lucky to have him standing in it.

When Brian Redmon's heart stopped beating during that church service a few years back, David responded by running to Brian. Most of the room intuitively backed away, but not David. Mercifully, he ran right to Brian and responded with every ounce of his being, precisely how God gifted him to act.

In the years I've known David, he has run into a burning house to make sure no one was in danger. I've seen him repeatedly drop everything he's doing and go to be with someone who was in the middle of their life blowing up. He has been beside me through the ups and downs of planting and leading a church. If you're looking for David, look for someone who is in trouble. David won't be far away.

When David's close friends lost their infant daughter to a tragic accident, David was right there beside their family. That level of grief is hard to bear. Most people who experience it notice that as time goes by, people stop calling. They stop dropping by. The suffering of someone deep in grief is a part of who they are, and most of us don't know what to say or do, so we don't say or do anything. Thank God for the gift of the Responders.

Some friends will talk to you when they have time; others will make time to speak with you. David is a makes-time friend. He will drop everything to be with someone who needs him, including me. Whether it's making a dump run with a truck packed full of stuff, or just hanging with me on a long journey to India because he knows how hard those trips are to make alone, David is present.

I hesitated to share this next part because the experience is recent that the trauma is so fresh and real. I hesitated because David is my friend, and I don't want to do anything that would bring pain to him and his family. But with his permission, I'm sharing what I know to be one of the most Responder moments I've ever witnessed and will ever witness this side of heaven.

David's daughter, Rebekah, passed away at the age of eighteen. All those years David ran to crises in others' lives, and he was suddenly the one in crisis. There's no way to adequately express the trauma, grief, and hurt David's family felt and continue to feel.

When it came time for the memorial service, David told me that he wanted to lead it. I thought that was a terrible idea. I felt like he needed the time to grieve. And by the way, he did grieve. He still grieves.

As a public speaker, I know the weight of giving a talk at a funeral for someone's child. It was impossible to imagine how David would be able to do this for Rebekah. I was afraid he wouldn't be able to get the words out in front of a packed room.

David recognized the risk he was taking. He wrote out word for word what he wanted to say. In the event he was unable to do so, I would read the comments for him. It would be my voice, but the words would be his.

As David and his wife, Jayna, entered the sanctuary at the beginning of the service, he could barely walk. The grief was suffocating. The sanctuary was packed, and there were many more in an overflow room. Rebekah was loved by so many. As David took the stage, another pastor and I walked with him and were seated on his right and left. We were positioned just behind where he was going to stand. We were there to catch him if he fell.

But something supernatural happened that day. David, the Responder, caught us. He caught every person in that room. He stood up and shared every single word he had on his heart.

David indeed needed to grieve, but he also needed to give his gift. The thing he needed the most at that moment was to be who we needed him to be. We needed a Responder, and he was there for us.

As our missions pastor, a community figure, and the father of a daughter whose heartbroken friends needed comfort, David responded to our sorrow. Reading this, you might think David's stance was unhealthy. In all honesty, leading up to that moment, I wondered the same thing. But I watched that man stand up in front of a packed church and be the gospel to everyone there.

I've seen other parents stand and share at funerals for their children. They were all inspiring in their own way. But I've never seen anything like I did that day. I hope I never have to see it again. But in those moments, God reached through the conduit of David Christopher, the Responder, and brought comfort and healing to every single person in that room.

A PICTURE OF THE GOSPEL

Jesus told a story that we now know as the "Good Samaritan." A man lay bleeding and dying, and nobody would stop to help him. The one man who did stop is known only as "a Samaritan."

Plenty of intense theological jargon exists about the priest and a Pharisee, who should have stopped.

But take a deeper dive, and you see there was more going on. A Samaritan in Jesus' day was considered an outsider, neither Jew nor Gentile. He was overlooked and left out. Responders struggle with that very thing. In a vulnerable moment, they'll tell you they feel like they're outside looking in, their dreams just out of reach. Maybe it's through the window of their pain that they see so clearly the pain of others. They know what it feels like to be left alone.

A.W. Tozer once wrote, "It is doubtful whether God can bless a man greatly until he has hurt him deeply."[7] I don't know if that's true for everyone, but it's certainly true of Responders.

This Samaritan man didn't just stop, didn't just throw money at the man. He bent over and poured oil and wine into the wounds. He placed the wounded man on his donkey and took him to the nearest inn. He told the innkeeper that he would pay for the man's lodging. If the man incurred additional expenses for caretaking, the Samaritan would pay those when he returned. *Did you catch that?* This guy was coming back. Responders don't just run in and back out. They are with you for the long haul.

Responders are an incredible picture of the gospel. When we read the story of the good Samaritan, we want to believe that we would be like him. You may have even heard a sermon challenging you not to be the one who walks by. Are you the Levite who was in too much of a hurry? Are you the Pharisee who couldn't be bothered? Or are you the Samaritan who took the time to stop?

But there's one more character in this story: the man bleeding and dying was saved by a compassionate Responder. The wounded man symbolizes us—and Jesus paid the bill. He's going to return and anything else that we owe, He'll pay that too. That's Jesus, the ultimate Responder.

Every time David Christopher stops to see someone in pain and affliction, he is not preaching the gospel; he is the gospel. Thank God for Responders. Thank God for David.

A RESPONDER'S MENTOR: THE APOSTLE JOHN

Jesus had twelve disciples who were with him almost nonstop for the better part of three years. And yet, at His crucifixion, only one showed up—John. Judas was otherwise preoccupied, but the ten other disciples into whom Jesus poured His life were MIA.

It's easy to throw judgmental rocks at those guys, but if I'm uncomfortably honest, I might have been among those absent, hiding in the tall grass, so to speak. You see, there was a significant risk in showing up for Jesus when bloody hell had broken loose. The same people who were hammering spikes into the hands and feet of Jesus could've easily aimed their anger, malice, and sharp tools at any of his followers in the vicinity. Running toward Jesus in His moment of crisis was perilous. Their safety wasn't guaranteed. Jesus would die surrounded by people, but all alone.

And yet, there was John. When the other disciples took off, John sprinted toward him. Physically, John could do nothing, but still, he was there. As the day wore on and death was about to wrench his last breath, Jesus looked at John and asked him to take care of Mary, his mother. While we have no record of what happened to Joseph (the Bible makes no mention of him past Jesus' adolescence), the assumption is that he had died, and Mary was a widow.

From the cross, Jesus told John, "This is your mother." Jesus recognized the Responder gift in John. He knew John was someone who wouldn't just show up for the moment; he would stay for the journey no matter how blasted hard it was, flying shrapnel be damned. Once the initial shock and sadness began to wear off, someone would need to stay. It wasn't because John was the only disciple, and Jesus didn't have any other option. It was because John wasn't going anywhere, and he was the best option.

When news reached the other disciples that Jesus' body wasn't in the tomb, Peter and John ran to the burial chamber. Scripture states that John ran ahead. He was the first one there. He and Peter didn't know what had happened. To them, the most likely scenario was that thieves had stolen Jesus' body, and perhaps those behind the body-snatch lingered. John ran toward significant personal risk. Arriving first at the tomb wasn't merely winning a race; John was responding to a crisis.

Responders aren't weak or wimpy, and John was no exception. James and his brother boldly asked Jesus if they should call down fire on those who had rejected Jesus in Samaria when they were on their way to Jerusalem. Jesus gave John the nickname "son of thunder." John did not vacate his gift of mercy in that defining moment. Instead, he was incredibly merciful to his friend Jesus. The folks in question were abusing Jesus. Responders do not like bullies.

John's writings offer the most significant clues regarding his Responder gift. There are four New Testament Gospels. Matthew, Mark, and Luke are the synoptic Gospels because they synthesize the life of Jesus so well. The Gospel of John stands out as a completely different type of Gospel. It's unique to the New Testament. That's such a Responder move. The epistles of John read like the words of a Responder. He spoke of love. He challenged: If you see your neighbor in need and have the means to help and do nothing, "how can you say you have the love of God in you?" (1 John 3:17)

And then there's the Book of Revelation. I can't think of a more Responder piece of literature than those twenty-two chapters. Most modern readers are confused by this book; it's scary and hard to believe. However, those who originally received and read these writings embraced them as words of comfort and hope for a church in dire straits. Jesus knew an afflicted church would need the gift of a Responder. While your King James Bible might call him John the Revelator, we know he was more than that. He was John the Responder.

RECOGNIZING A RESPONDER

Responders are usually easy to spot. There's something in them that drives a need to be unique and stand out. Their clothing isn't the standard blue jeans and tennis shoes. Especially in males, there's unique jewelry involved such as rings, chain necklaces, or chain wallets. I'm speaking in generalizations, but if you see someone showing up dressed and adorned like no one else in the room, that's a clue you're looking at a Responder.

Responders can come on strong. Their love language is time, and their idea of a good time is sitting for hours in deep conversation. Their gift of mercy is the gift of time—going deep with someone, pressing in for the relationship. A Responder is not going to have multiplied friendships that are a mile wide and an inch deep because the gift requires strength, perseverance, and depth.

Responders are similar to Collaborators; they are willing to jump in and help at a moment's notice. The two gifts are often confused with each other. Here's the main difference: A Collaborator will be moving at lightspeed, mapping all of the practical things needed to complete a task. A Responder might deal with the practical stuff, but the primary focus is not what needs to be done as much as who needs it done. One is Martha; the other is Mary. And the world needs both.

In the immediate aftermath of a tragedy, many people show up, but Responders hang around for the long haul. They're a necessary and ongoing part of the recovery process. They stick around. The gift of mercy is a gift of presence—of being there—and staying there.

The Apostle Paul specifically commanded those with the gift of mercy to deliver the gift "cheerfully" (Romans 12:8). There is a deep well of wisdom in Paul's command because those who feel others' pain can feel it so intensely, they may want to invoke the scorch of fire on an oppressor. At the same time, spending time with those who are experiencing trauma can take a toll. Sitting with someone in their trauma affects you as well. Responders must be self-aware and draw boundaries for their own mental and emotional health. This gift is not for sissies.

On the downside, Responders tend to withdraw in the day-to-day life of a relationship. In the absence of a crisis, Responders will pull back if they aren't getting back what they give in relationships. They have such active imaginations that they create storylines in their minds of what others are doing or thinking to hurt them. Most times, the constructed narratives are untrue, but to Responders, they feel entirely real. They use this narrative to justify the pulling back, leaving the person in the dark.

Responders feel deeply, which is a blessing and a curse. They will find themselves in situations where the mercy they are giving isn't appreciated. Rejection is harsh for anyone, but for Responders, it can seem overwhelming.

This gift of mercy so inherent in Responders comes at a high cost to those entrusted to deliver it. Somewhere along the way, Satan whispers in the Responder's ear, "You don't fit in." Thus, many Responders fear abandonment.

No doubt about it, responding can be a lonely gift because it's not often reciprocated. Those who give so much often receive little. That's the price many pay for the honor of being blessed with this rare gift. God specifically chose those who would and could deliver it. It's a privilege and an honor.

THE SEVEN WORKING TOGETHER

A **Visionary** offers big picture thinking to a Responder who so often focuses on immediate needs. If Responders are left to their own imaginations, they might never move on dreams or ideas. Visionaries have a way of nudging them out of the fog.

A **Collaborator** helps keep the ball rolling for the Responder by managing the practical step-by-step stuff. Responders can get slowed down because they prefer to work alone. Collaborators help with bringing substance and workforce to the Responder.

A **Discerner** brings clarity to the Responder in making decisions because a Responder is all soul and will respond to stories that may or may not be true. When a Responder is dreaming, a Discerner helps them ground in reality.

An **Encourager** is a vital B-12 shot for a Responder who feels the pain and suffering others. It's not that Responders need cheering up; they need to be cheered on. An Encourager is a beautiful picture of this.

An **Imparter** conveys strength to a Responder who may become depleted by giving so much to others. Imparters can sense when Responders have poured themselves out and need refreshment.

A **Guardian** protects details and data, enabling a Responder to function wisely. Responders need Guardians to handle the details their dreams require.

Are you a Responder?

Part III

Develop Your Gift

"Do not neglect your gift, which was given you through prophecy when the body of elders laid their hands on you."

–1 Timothy 4:14; NIV

Chapter 12

Who Has Your Reins?

"For thou hast possessed my reins: thou hast covered me in my mother's womb."

– Psalm 139:13; KJV

The Power of the Seven

THE POWER OF THE SEVEN

Y DAUGHTERS WON THE DNA LOTTERY. They look like their mom. This likeness is a good thing because I've seen myself in the mirror.

As children of God, we favor our Father, and the seven gifts—strands of His DNA—are in us. Jesus carried God's *imago dei* (as His body and care for humankind) to earth. As the body of Christ—brothers and sisters of Jesus—we have the same privilege.

You are the conduit of a specific gift from God. He encoded your gift while you were in the womb. It's your part of the body of Christ—a representation of Him on earth. You are not God, but you are His child—and the equivalent of God's DNA lives within you. It's the cosmic version of "she has her Father's eyes."

That reality makes you an existential threat to the kingdom of darkness. You are a walking, talking, living child of God moving around in a world where Satan has power for the time being. He wants to stop you, so there's a vigorous, ongoing war to control your gift. Satan wants to neutralize it.

Don't underestimate the intensity of this battle because the stakes are high. When you grasp this, the kingdom of God advances. For example, deploying the seven gifts to bring clean water to African children is an assault on Satan's plans because he wants to kill them.

To understand Satan's strategy for neutralizing your gift, first, understand God's original intentions for it. The King James translation of the Bible usually loses me at "thee, thou, and verily," but its wording in Psalm 139:13 captivates my attention: "For thou hast possessed my reins: thou hast covered me in my mother's womb." Most scholars who translate modern Bible versions change "possessed my reins" to "created my inmost being." Why? Perhaps they've never experienced the power of a slim leather strap to control a two-thousand-pound horse.

You can ride a horse without a saddle, but you're in big trouble without reins, and so is the horse. However, when you harness a horse's strength through wise reining, the huge beast becomes a muscular change agent.

The Bible uses that same imagery: "When we put bits into the mouths of horses to make them obey us, we can turn the whole animal" (James 3:3; NIV). There's a truth in this that can change your life. This is Holy Spirit transformation.

Don't miss the integral message of Psalm 139:13! You have a God-given gift—and when properly harnessed—when Jesus possesses the reins of that gift, the body of Christ is strengthened and creates awe-inspiring good in the world. That's the result God wants!

Satan has other plans. Your gift, when not submitted to God, will send you smashing into the rocks. The gift that is meant to create joy and impact the world for good will instead burn your life down. A horse prodded by an inexperienced or cruel rider will keep sprinting as long as the rider keeps prodding. Together, the two will run themselves to death.

THE GIFT TRIP OF FEAR

If God doesn't control the reins in your life, your gift can trip you up big time. I know all about this. When my daughter, Madi, was a preschooler, I used to take her to a McDonald's Playland every Saturday morning. We called it Daddy-Madi time. In my mind, I was proactively doing what my father never did with me—spend time with his kid.

On those Saturday mornings, this Discerner dad would read and synthesize *The Tennessean* newspaper while Madi played. She would disappear into the tunnels, making intermittent appearances to wave at me while I drank coffee and caught up on what was going on in the Middle East and Murfreesboro.

Here's the harsh reality: I was there without being there. My body was on that playground, but my heart was not. I was emulating behavior I experienced as a young boy—withdrawal. My dad drove off in a pickup truck; I drove off in a newspaper. Madi deserved and wanted my full attention, but she didn't get it. I cringe to think of the joys I missed on those Saturday mornings because I had my nose stuck in a newspaper when my heart could have engaged with my little girl.

What drove me to withdraw into newsprint? God didn't possess my inner man. Satan used fear, one of his trademarks, to control my reins. Because of my childhood's wounds, which told me I didn't matter or know how to connect, I was fearful of connecting with others, even my little girl. None of this was conscious; I was completely unaware. And yet the damage was done to my baby girl.

As a Discerner, I have a core desire to be helpful and competent. It causes me to want to learn and absorb information continually. But where Madi was concerned, the fear that I didn't know how to connect neutralized my gift's strength. My daughter needed to know she had her daddy's heart. I was sitting there thinking I was father of the year because I took Madi to McDonald's. However, because my gift reins were in the wrong hands, my thirst for knowledge kept me in my head—and that left Madi out. My uncontrolled gift was building a wall between us. Fear doesn't draw us together; it tears us apart. Remember, in the Garden of Eden, when God found Adam hiding? Adam's response was, "I was afraid, so I hid" (Genesis 3:10).

When this Discerner steers toward isolation and detachment, it's the equivalent of shipwrecking into an island of fear and loneliness. I'm not alone in this vulnerability. Satan can use fear to yank the reins of all seven members and thus disintegrate what God wants to integrate, weakening the body of Christ. Here's his gambit for each of the other gifts:

Visionary: Satan uses fear to seize your desire for value and success and cause you to focus on accomplishing your goals for praise at the cost of being available to those you love.

Collaborator: Satan uses fear to overtake your desire for love and acceptance, steering you toward serving others in a desperate attempt to be loved and wanted.

Encourager: Satan uses fear to usurp your desire for contentment and excitement and pivot you away from commitments or scheduling in a desire to not miss out on last-minute opportunities—especially if you think a situation is keeping you from a more exciting experience.

Imparter: Satan uses fear to capture your core desire for internal peace by avoiding conflict, adapting to others' preferences rather than stating your own, and losing yourself in the process.

Guardian: Satan uses fear to commandeer your desire for personal support and stability, and presses you toward expecting the worst, losing yourself in overthinking decisions, trapping yourself in analysis paralysis.

Responder: Satan uses fear to hijack your desire to positively impact the world and push you toward feeling misunderstood, causing you to double down on being unique and creative at the expense of isolating yourself.

THE WEAPON OF SHAME

If fear is the wound, Satan's most effective weapon is toxic shame. Toxic shame doesn't say, "I did something wrong." It screams, "I am something wrong." That toxicity isolates based on the belief, "It's only me, and if anyone ever really knew the real me, they would leave me."

This kind of shame is so insidious that you not only carry it for things you've done, but also for injustice done to you. It's a shocking fact that the shame felt by a victim of trauma is carried in the same place as if that person had committed the trauma. It's why a sexually abused woman will so often blame herself: "I should have..." This shame is why sexually abused children will often not tell their caregivers. They feel ashamed.

This is deep and painful stuff, but I hope you'll stay with me. Jesus truly wants to heal this part of you, to take the reins of your life once again so your gift can run free.

A young child intuitively knows a caregiver is the lifeline, the only hope for survival—food, water, and safety. When a child is ignored or experiences a caregiver's anger, shame lands on that young heart. The child knows something's wrong, but the core desire is to maintain that connection.

In the heart of young children, it's terrifying to think something is wrong with the caregiver. They couldn't properly articulate it, but the feeling is that if there is something wrong with this person who is supposed to love and care for me, then I'm on my own, and that means I'm in deep trouble. It's not conscious; it's visceral. And so terrifying that it's easier for the child to think there's something wrong with him or her. So, toxic shame sets in—and performance to maintain or regain connection begins. This shame is why even in horrible abusive situations, a child being removed from an abusive caregiver will often hold on to that person, crying to stay.

The part of your soul that carries shame doesn't differentiate the lines as clearly as you'd think. A victim of abuse is just that, a victim. But the soul holds on to it in the same shame-filled place.

No wonder Jesus went to the cross, despising shame (Hebrews 12:1-3). You would think that He would've gone to the cross abhorring the physical pain or the injustice, but it was the shame He despised. Satan has artfully weaponized shame since the tragedy in the Garden of Eden, and it's still a primary tool in his war against you and your gift.

Do you see how feelings, such as fear and shame, can take control of your gift and steer you away from God's best for your life? It's time to give the reins of your life to God. How do you do that? Turn the page, and let's begin the fight for your gift.

Chapter 13

The Wounded Healer

"Do not conform to the pattern of this world,
but be transformed by the renewing of your mind."

– Romans 12:2; NIV

ON THE DAY MY DAD FLATLINED, I was eight years old and parked in a waiting room at the VA Hospital in Omaha. The room reeked of bleach and urine. Despite the obnoxious smell, my brothers and I were hungry and wondering why our grandparents hadn't delivered on a McDonald's promise. Omaha meant a Happy Meal for four boys who lived in a small town three hours away.

We hadn't seen our dad in the months since he went into the hospital for a mystery illness. Earlier on the promised McDonald's day, they rolled a man Mom said was our dad into the waiting room to see us. To me, it looked like someone had unzipped Dad and pulled this guy out. He was a frail and vacuous caricature of my father. There were no hugs; it wasn't a reunion moment that would go viral on the internet. I don't recall anything spoken. My brothers and I just stood there, fidgeting in our sneakers on a sticky floor that smelled like a bleach bottle took a piss.

After a few moments, the medical staff wheeled Dad back to the elevator. Somewhere along the way, he went into cardiac arrest and flatlined. After several endless hours, when I eventually no longer noticed the waiting room's smell, my mother and grandfather reappeared. They said nothing to us about Dad dying on the gurney or the doctors who brought him back to life. There was no hint that something traumatic had happened. We just loaded up in the car and went to McDonald's. A lot of serious crap had gone down, and Mom and Grandad glossed right over it. I'm sure they didn't want to upset us. But they even didn't say, "We're sorry, boys, but Daddy was a little sicker than we thought." There was nothing except ordering four Happy Meals at McDonald's with no sense of irony.

When I was in my teens and learned the truth about that day, I was stunned and hurt. But I never said a word. We boys learned early on that we didn't talk about things like that. It was best to mop over such stuff. Spray deodorizer to mask the stench, and when you do that long enough, you eventually don't notice the smell anymore.

Without my father being healthy enough to care for our family, and no work for my mother in our small rural town, I received a wounding message that my parents never once spoke: *You're on your own, Darren. No one is coming for you. No whining. Keep your angst to yourself.*

As an adult, my wound drove me to launch companies and create jobs. I was on my own, using my Discerner mind to provide jobs and healthcare benefits. I knew what it was like not to have those things and didn't want others to go through what I did. Wounds can drive each of us to accomplish bad and good things. I was fortunate that my wounds bled into an addiction to work and not alcohol or drugs. Whatever the addiction, it's just a way of numbing pain, a form of mopping over what lies beneath.

WOUNDS THAT THWART THE SEVEN GIFTS

Before you check the book jacket to ensure you're still reading *The Power of the Seven* and not the confessions of a pastor in therapy, get this message: *childhood wounds can radically thwart the discovery, development, and delivery of the seven gifts. Satan knows this all too well.*

That wound from my childhood caused me to retreat into the mindset that it was not okay to be emotionally transparent in this world. It was a wound Satan wanted to use to neutralize my Discerner gift. And for years, he did a bang-up job. (Fair warning, Satan is intent on neutralizing your gift too.)

Psychologists have all kinds of names for childhood traumas. Counselors call them *wounding childhood messages.* Freud talked about them in terms of *repression*. The Bible calls this wounding being "conformed to the pattern of this world" (Romans 12:2). To me, that tag best sums up the problem.

The message isn't that you're conforming yourself, but that the world is molding you to its patterns. Children are remarkable observers and terrible interpreters. Nobody ever told me I was on my own. My parents did the best they could with the tools their parents gave them. Your parents raised you using toolkits inherited from their parents. (Jesus might be in your heart, but your grandfather is in your bones.) There's a pattern that your parents or caregivers learned, and they, in turn, conformed you to that pattern, either explicitly or implicitly. The older your children get, the more you begin to see yourself in them. And, unless you are the first perfect parent since the Garden of Eden, that includes the wounds you've inflicted on your children.

The conformity pattern is the design Satan revels in and uses to cripple you and thwart your God-given gift. Satan's superpower isn't voodoo or witchcraft or scary ghosts. It's lies. It has always been lies. And Satan knows the most powerful weapon he has is a lie embedded deep in your soul.

We carry our childhood wounds throughout life. Ephesians 6:16 refers to them as "fiery darts of the enemy." Satan's power emanates from the lies he uses to jab our wounds and keep them infected and oozing dysfunction. When he wounded Adam and Eve in the Garden of Eden, it wasn't with magic; it was with lies. The lies of the garden continue to this day: "Did God really say?"

We all have wounds embedded in our hearts. Those wounds might flesh out differently from person to person, but the messages of those wounds—the lies of the enemy (those fiery darts)—hit the seven gifts in commonplace ways.

Visionary: "It's not okay to be vulnerable and trusting."
Collaborator: "It's not okay to have your own needs."
Discerner: "It's not okay to be comfortable in the world."
Encourager: "It's not okay to depend on anyone for anything."
Imparter: "It's not okay to assert yourself."
Guardian: "It's not okay to make mistakes."
Responder: "It's not okay to be too functional or happy."

These are the wounds Satan has used for millennia to impede the power of the seven. They are the pattern of this world. Every version of "Did God really say?" falls into one of these categories.

HEALING THE WOUNDS

That's a lot of heavy stuff, but here's the incredible news: "By His stripes, you are healed."

Isaiah 53:5 makes it clear that God wants to heal our childhood wounds and transform them into spiritual gifts that change the world. Did you catch that? God wants to take what Satan means for harm and use it for good! Nothing is wasted. The pain you and I have suffered isn't for nothing. God can transform us!

The goodness of God wants to heal us from being conformed (surrendered) to that pattern of childhood wounds and instead transform us (change us from the inside out) into Christ-followers who do the good, perfect, and pleasing will of God by maximizing our gifts through the power of the seven. This transformation is vital to doing God's will on earth "as it is in heaven."

The promise of Romans 8:28 is simple. "In all things, He is working for the good of those who love Him and are called according to His purpose." That's not a promise that for every bad thing, you get one good thing. God reveals the good He is working for in our lives. In Romans 8:29, we read, "For those God foreknew, he also predestined *to be conformed to the image of His Son.*"

This verse communicates that in all things, God is transforming you into the image of His Son. At least in part, the "image of His Son" refers to how you represent a picture of Jesus to this world. It's the gift God gave you discovered, developed, and delivered to the world. *The Holy Spirit's power of transformation turns wounds into gifts.* That's a story as old as time. Joseph's message to his brothers in Genesis 29 was that what they did to harm him, God used for good.

Each one of us has a gift "according to the grace He has given us." The grace given to us is the healing that He wants to do in us so that our gifts shine. Being transformed into the image of Jesus isn't nebulous and ethereal. It's quite specific, and transformation flowing through the seven gifts means you reflect a specific part of who Jesus is.

A Visionary's transformation will reflect Jesus as someone who turned over tables when it was time to turn them over, but also who stopped long enough for His friends to catch up.

A Collaborator's transformation will reflect Jesus as someone who serves others' needs as Christ did—because He loved them—not to get love from them.

A transformed Encourager will reflect Jesus and be less afraid of the painful and sad parts of life, rejoicing with those who rejoice and weeping with them.

The transformation for an Imparter is a journey toward looking more like Jesus the Imparter—one who is careful with words, but not silent, one who brings peace to stormy situations.

Jesus is the ultimate Guardian, and a Guardian's transformation leads that person to look more like Jesus. The lie that you can't trust yourself, that you're not safe? When it's healed, that fear doesn't paralyze a Guardian; it energizes. What once kept a Guardian frozen in a corner empowers action.

A Responder's transformation leads to reflecting Jesus the Responder. Out of love, He moved with compassion toward those who were hurting and not out of a fear of being rejected.

And a Discerner like me? Well, Jesus, the consummate Discerner, taught like one who had authority, but He also spoke from his heart with his friends and family. That's what transformation does for a Discerner.

Paul revealed quite clearly how transformation occurs: "By the renewing of your mind." The word *mind* in Romans 12:2 is the synonym for the soul. God wants to renew all the nooks and crannies of our tattered souls. The Holy Spirit does the heavy lifting; you and I do the daily submitting. This transformation isn't a magic pill or snap of the finger. Soul transformation transpires a little at a time. That means, like me, you're going to need to give yourself the same grace God the Father offers.

The Apostle Paul knew the transformational journey all too well. When you read his words in Romans 7, you realize he wrestled with conformity, just like the rest of us: "Why do I do the things I don't want to do?" Those are the words of a man desperate for transformation, which takes time. Like Paul, you're going to blow it along the way. There will be days you'll feel like Paul when he said, "What a wretched man I am! Who will rescue me from this body that is subject to death? Thanks be to God, who delivers me through Jesus Christ, our Lord (Romans 7:24-25). In those moments when you're living out of your wound and not your healing, Paul's words offer hope: "There is therefore now no condemnation to those who are in Christ Jesus."

Do you think Paul might have had some wounds to overcome? Before Christ, he spent every waking hour of his life persecuting, arresting and killing Christians. You don't have to be a genius to realize Paul was dealing with some profound wounds of his own. Hurt people, hurt people.

After his miraculous conversion to Jesus, can you imagine the shame Paul must have carried? The family and friends of people he killed were those to whom he later wrote letters. How do you face someone when you unjustly executed their loved one?

The message of being transformed by the renewing of your mind wasn't just a nice theory for Paul; he was living proof. The wounds that drove Paul to persecute and kill Christians were the soul gashes God healed and used to transform Paul into the Visionary who would launch the church! If God can transform Paul, He can transform you and me.

Gospel Motivation

When Paul talked about transformation, he didn't speak about psychology or techniques. He focused solely on what transformed him: the gospel of Jesus. The gospel tells us Jesus personally experienced the things that wounded you and me. The statement, "He was wounded for our transgressions," is full of meaning because, on the cross, Jesus experienced a reverse transformation: "He who knew no sin, became sin." Jesus transformed from healed to wounded. He went through the ultimate transformation of light to darkness so we can go through the ultimate transformation from darkness to light. On the cross, Jesus bore every wounding childhood message. And these wounds correspond to the seven gifts.

For the Visionary, whose wound is that you can't trust anyone, Jesus experienced ultimate betrayal of his friend Judas, who sold him out for thirty pieces of silver.

For the Collaborator, whose wound is that it's not okay to have your own needs, Jesus' needs were ignored entirely—no food or water. His clothing was stolen and auctioned.

For the Discerner, whose wound is that it's not okay to be comfortable in this world, that you're supposed to suffer, God the Father turned His back on Jesus, leaving Him cosmically alone.

For the Encourager, whose wound is that it's not okay to depend on anyone for anything, Jesus cried out, "My God, why have You forsaken me?"

For the Imparter, who has absorbed the message that it's not okay to assert yourself, Jesus was silent in the face of Pilate and his accusers.

For the Guardian, who feels it's not okay because no one sees me for who I really am, Jesus was rejected by those who should have seen and known.

For the Responder, whose wound is that it's not okay to be too functional or happy, Jesus on the cross cried out to God, "Why have You forsaken me?"

Jesus was wounded for our transgressions. Those wounds were physical and emotional. The gospel tells us that it was through those wounds that we can experience healing. Jesus died for those wounds on the cross so that we can experience the transformation of our wounds from darkness to light.

Like Paul, my transformation journey continues day by day, step by step. And, so can yours. Through forgiveness and the day-by-day transformation of the Holy Spirit, the healing of your wounds liberates you to develop your gift and deliver it to a world in desperate need of the DNA of Jesus.

Chapter 14

Stay in Your Lane

"So since we find ourselves fashioned into all these excellently formed and marvelously functioning parts in Christ's body, let's just go ahead and be what we were made to be, without enviously or pridefully comparing ourselves with each other, or trying to be something we aren't."

– Romans 12:4-6; MSG

The Power of the Seven

E MBRACING YOUR GIFT gives you glorious freedom, but often we look at the bounty of the seven gifts and resist being restricted to one. I hate to sound like a parent, but the adage, "It's for your own good," definitely applies here.

When I stay in my lane as a Discerner, leading Conduit is a joy and a privilege. When I switch lanes to try and lead like a Visionary, it's exhausting. If I attempt to maneuver like a Collaborator or a Responder, everyone around me gets frustrated. And if I tried to act like an Encourager? Well, it would not be pretty.

On the flip side, it's frustrating for those around me when I expect them to lead a specific ministry or endeavor the way I would do it. The greatest freedom you and I can experience is the freedom to stay in God's respective lanes for us.

Are there standards and practices that are important regardless of the gift? Absolutely. But that's not what I'm talking about. For instance, it's important to be prompt for a meeting, especially when others are involved. Promptness doesn't flow naturally for Encouragers or Responders as it does for Guardians and Discerners, but it's important. The gifts don't support the age-old excuse, "That's just who I am; deal with it." On the other hand, the knowledge that a Responder or Encourager might struggle with promptness allows for some empathy from others.

The beauty of the power of the seven is that I don't have to be every gift of Romans 12 as I'm leading my church. That attempt has led to the burnout of many church leaders. Sure, there's the temptation for me to look down the road at Pastor Mark Rampulla, a killer Encourager, and want to be like him. I can look at how detail-oriented my Guardian friend Pastor Charlie Weir is and feel woefully unorganized. When I talk to my friend Pastor John Breland, a keen Visionary, it's tempting to feel my leadership is nearsighted. But the drive to be someone God didn't create me to be is bondage, not freedom! Freedom is staying in my lane—the lane God designed for me. Freedom is not overwhelming myself with trying to be all the best parts of everyone I know. That's a trap Satan sets. That's bondage.

DON'T FEEL THE BURN

It's critical—and simultaneously freeing—for all of us to stay in our God-given lanes. Staying in my lane as a pastor is central not only to my well-being but also for those leading ministries inside our church family.

Jim Henderson has been with me at Conduit since before the church was born. He is an Imparter and was instrumental in bringing me peace that God had called me to plant a church. He and I were sitting at a coffee shop, reconnecting after losing touch for a couple of years, and about midway through, Jim said, "If you're ever ready to hang out a shingle, start a church, and be the pastor, I'll be your kids' guy."

I wish Jim had given me a heads-up before making that statement. That coffee was way too expensive for the spit-take that I did. I'd been alive for thirty-eight years at that point, and no one had ever suggested I should plant a church. That same week, Shannon and I had finally submitted to the call to plant a church in the Nashville area. We had not told a soul.

It wasn't just that Jim said it; it was the way he said it. Jim, the Imparter, was bringing peace to the stormy sea I was stepping onto. He was offering to step into the boat with us. He wasn't giving me a "you can do it" speech. That wasn't what I needed. He was giving me the "it's going to be okay" gift of peace that naturally flows from an Imparter.

At the time, Jim served a church where the pastor shot down his ideas and retrained his methodology. The pastor there is a good man who loves the Lord. But the practice of forcing Jim into a leadership box that censured his Imparter gift left my friend feeling frustrated and unappreciated.

Often, when you're frustrated in a role or job, it's because your gift is restricted. The church pastor where Jim was serving was trying to steer Jim into a lane Jim didn't have the God-given ability to navigate. He was making the common mistake of forcing Jim to mimic the pastor's gift instead of making room for Jim to deliver his own.

Jim went on to lead Conduit's children's ministry, and later on, our youth group. The primary job description? "Be Jim to as many kids as you can." As a Discerner, I would've led the children's ministry quite differently than Jim. It would've been many thought-provoking conversations, digging deep into theological concepts about how science and the Bible relate. Doesn't that sound like a blast for teenagers? Don't answer that.

How does an Imparter lead students? Well, kids are tons of fun—creative, and filled with high energy. Jim dreamed up and curated huge events the kids loved. But it wasn't just the big events; it was the hands-on ministry that made the difference. Jim's Imparter gift spotted kids on the fringe who didn't fit in. He made sure they felt included and seen. He inspired confidence in parents that their kids were well-loved. Jim poured his soul into the youth, imparting peace to those fighting anxiety.

Imparters aren't known for command of the details. For that matter, neither are Discerners. What to do about that? Add a Guardian to the mix. Jim's wife, Donna, is a textbook Guardian. She is by training a science teacher—and a darn good one. Donna is one of the smartest people I know. She has a command of the details in a way that Imparters don't. Jim's ideas and events needed someone who could keep it on the rails. Donna made sure budgets were respected, and supplies ordered. She worked beside Jim protecting the vision and integrity of the ministry. Jim also had individuals with the other five gifts involved with his ministry. As they traveled in their lanes, a life-changing student ministry was born.

Our student ministry would've looked 100 percent different if God had called a Responder or Visionary to lead it, but He didn't. Inviting Jim to stay in his lane and deliver his Imparter gift greatly benefited the students while allowing Jim to be himself.

When you know who God wired you to be, staying in your lane isn't all that hard. There are career paths and callings that should be avoided by specific gifts. A job or ministry that requires running numbers on a computer five days a week will quickly suffocate a Responder. Likewise, a Guardian isn't the first choice when a situation requires copious mercy and a tender bedside manner. A Collaborator might not be the best person to handle a role that requires detaching emotionally and making decisions based on hardcore facts. And a Discerner should avoid a role that requires executing a mission from beginning to end. I am living proof of this. Just ask my Collaborator wife.

In our modern context, the pressure to be everyone at all times is mind-numbing. And the amount of energy required to fake unowned gifts is soul-crushing. Every mission calls for all the gifts on some level. We need to be ourselves, but we desperately need one another. That's the uplifting and unifying power of the seven.

Staying in your gift lane also creates empathy. When Jim didn't handle something the way I would've handled it, I was able to take a breath and think, of course, he didn't. It's not that Jim and I didn't challenge each other to be better, more free versions of ourselves. But understanding our gifts gave us understanding and empathy when we handled stuff differently.

CONFUSING THE MINISTRY AND THE GIFT

An entire industry has sprung up around training leaders, and this includes church leaders. Often when you hear the phrasing, "This is how you should lead," it's a list of what a Visionary would do. Sure, there are universal leadership principles and skills. But don't confuse those principles with your gift. For example, don't use your gift as an excuse not to deal with conflict if you're a Discerner. But also, don't take on shame if clear communication doesn't come as natural to you if you're a Responder.

The quickest way to burnout is to confuse the ministry and the gift. I'm convinced that much of what we call burnout in modern church circles is symptomatic of people not delivering the gifts God created them to give. It could be that the leader of a particular church thinks the way he's wired is the way everyone in the church is supposed to lead. So, a Visionary pastor might demand his team lead their areas the way he would. And that's a big mistake. It's confusing mission with gifting. The church has a mission, and it's essential to get everyone to agree and be on the same page in that mission while simultaneously allowing individuals to use their gifts to accomplish the mission.

The Message interpretation of Romans 12:4-6 hits this truth on the head: "So since we find ourselves fashioned into all these excellently formed and marvelously functioning parts in Christ's body, let's just go ahead and be what we were made to be, without enviously or pridefully comparing ourselves with each other, or trying to be something we aren't."

The first time I taught this truth at Conduit Church, I had arranged for someone to bring me a glass of water while I was teaching. I had him dramatically trip and fall, spilling the water and shattering the glass. Then I just stood back and watched.

The Responders immediately ran to him to make sure the guy was okay. The Collaborators leaped to their feet, running for the broom and mop. The Imparters sensed the discomfort of those around them and proceeded to calm the tension in the room. The Visionaries just stood there, envisioning a future where the trip didn't happen. Guardians were immediately looking for what specifically caused the fall and how to prevent a repeat. The Encouragers were giving the "Man, you're going to be fine" speech. And this Discerner was just fascinated with how the body of Christ works together so seamlessly.

Below the surface, a Guardian might look at an Encourager and wonder *Why aren't you fixing the corner of the rug that's sticking up? Don't you know that's dangerous?* A Collaborator might get frustrated that the Responder isn't grabbing a mop to help clean up the mess.

Asking, "Why don't you just ... (insert how you would handle it)" demands others do what you would do. You're pushing them to deliver your gift, not theirs, asking them to veer into your lane. This mindset says that your way is the only way. Paul called this "thinking of yourself more highly than you should" (Romans 12:3).

So, please don't get the big head, my friend. Stay in your lane and allow others to stay in theirs. When you do, the road to effective ministry flows in God's direction.

DON'T HOLD BACK

The life-changing stuff God can do through you has an eternal impact. You have an enormous amount of latitude in how you steward your gift on earth, but when you use it as God designed it, the world around you lights up. Your Creator receives praise—and He gets a real kick out of you. That's the way this stuff works.

God gave you your gift—entrusted it to you—so you could pour it out to a world that desperately needs it. When you steward your gift well, you live Matthew 5:16 brilliantly: "Let your light shine before men that they may see your good works and glorify God."

That verse means, "Don't hold back!" As Romans 12 co-workers, we function as a network, stewarding our gifts together for optimal results, covering the world with the hope, love, and light of Christ. Together, we can do amazing things with our gifts. That's exhilarating when you think about it! That's the power of the seven!

The greatest use of our gifts is to serve others; the Bible is clear about that. So, don't hold back! Holding back your gift isn't being a faithful steward of it. That would be like owning a new iPhone but leaving it in the box because you're afraid you'll drop it in the toilet. Holding back because you fear rejection or failure is simply not being a good curator of the gift God put inside of you, especially these days when the world is so dark.

Now, more than ever, we need to steward our gifts in one robust network of grace. The instruction manual for this is found in 1 Peter 4:7-11:

> *"The end of all things is near. Therefore, be alert and of sober mind so that you may pray. Above all, love each other deeply, because love covers over a multitude of sins. Offer hospitality to one another without grumbling. Each of you should use whatever gift you have received to serve others, as faithful stewards of God's grace in its various forms. If anyone speaks, they should do so as one who speaks the very words of God. If anyone serves, they should do so with the strength God provides, so that in all things God may be praised through Jesus Christ. To him be the glory and the power for ever and ever." (NIV)*

Those are dynamic, straightforward words. The message is crystal clear: As Christ-followers, we are to use our spiritual gifts to serve others. We are to work together in a network of love and light up the world for Him—hands held high, hearts in unison. That's the simple truth of the power of the seven.

IS IT SAFE?

God could've chosen any one of a million ways to bring His will to earth. He could have sneezed stars if He wanted. But the Creator of the universe chose us to implement His will.

I can sense the questions forming in your mind. This all sounds so risky. *What if I'm rejected? What if I try to do something, and it fails?* The question behind those questions is this: Is it safe? Remember the vignette from the C.S. Lewis classic *The Lion, The Witch and the Wardrobe?*

> *"Aslan is a lion—the Lion, the great Lion."*
> *"Ooh," said Susan. "I'd thought he was a man. Is he– quite safe? I shall feel rather nervous about meeting a lion."* ...
>
> *"Safe?" said Mr. Beaver... "Who said anything about safe?... 'Course he isn't safe. But he's good. He's the King, I tell you."*[8]

Jesus told us. "...and they shall never perish; no one will snatch them out of my hand" (John 10:28). The Jesus who gave you as a gift to the church is the same Jesus who continues to hold you in His hands. And maybe He's not safe by human standards, but He's good. The nail scars in his palms are proof of His goodness.

It's been said there's only one thing in heaven that's human-made: the scars on Jesus' body. He could've chosen to have those removed. But He didn't. He left them as proof that He's good, and we can trust Him. And there is no better place to be than living dangerously but safe in those strong, scarred hands. And that knowledge should light you up to stay in your gift lane and do amazing things for God as you partner with others.

Part IV

Deliver Your Gift

"God has given a spiritual gift to the church in you, and you dare not keep it to yourself."[9]

– Aaron Niequist

Chapter 15

Stop Sitting in Church

"How beautiful on the mountains are the feet of those who bring good news."

– Isaiah 52:7; NIV

The Power of the Seven

EVERY SUNDAY OF MY CHILDHOOD was spent butt-stuck on a hard, wooden church pew, trying to avoid my mom's arm smack. "Sit still!" She said, over and again. The long arm of the law had nothing on my mom's reach, who could somehow smack all four of her boys with one swing. Every smack and shush, along with stern stares from the preacher, instilled in me that church was a place to sit still and be quiet.

Years later, when this Discerner was making a lot of noise trying to figure out the Bible, a big revelation smacked me on the head: Jesus didn't go to all the trouble of death, burial, and resurrection so that I could sit quietly in church! The body of Christ is not supposed to sit still. The body of Christ is not supposed to be quiet. Instead, propelled by the seven's power, we are to move throughout our communities, our nation, and the world with bright lights and megaphones!

A CONDUIT OF HOPE

Jesus promised us that the "gates of hell shall not prevail" against His church. He didn't say that the gates of the church shall stand up against the attacks from hell. Jesus spoke of this battle as one in which we're on offense. We're not on a mission to protect the church; we're on a mission to attack hell. And the seven gifts reveal your place in the battleplan.

Sitting still is the last thing Jesus wants from any of us. He never said to "sit right there and wait till I get back." Instead, He used language like "occupy until I come." His invitation to follow Him implies He is going somewhere. For us, that means sitting is not an option.

Sure, children making noise can be distracting while someone is preaching a sermon. But be careful what you wish for. The sounds of children in a church are the echoes of life. If you stop hearing children, your church is dying. The sounds of the seven gifts echo action. If the primary goal is for everyone to sit still and be quiet for ninety minutes every week, then that church isn't dying; it's already dead.

Jesus gives us seven gifts, not to occupy our time, but to occupy enemy territory here on earth. This isn't busywork to distract us. We're an army occupying land until the King returns, not a child coloring the back of the bulletin until the sermon ends.

Each of us is one-seventh of the solution to anything Satan and his thugs' army can throw at us. And together? Well, we're unstoppable. God has gifted us to win! Jesus said He gave us the power to trample on serpents, scorpions, and the enemy's clout (Luke 10:19). That's treading on the power of the enemy, not sitting still on it. You tread on something so you can neutralize it and move beyond it.

God has called us to unite and pulverize the "devil's schemes" (Ephesians 6:13). Nothing motionless about that! Christianity is not a sitting-still faith. It's a snake-stomping, evil-overcoming, power-advancing, standing-firm, marching-forward, following-Jesus-right-to-the-gates-of-hell kind of faith. It's powerful faith. World-shifting stuff!

I believe this is the key to churches surviving and thriving into the next generation. If we fossilize into a country club, we will be competing with actual country clubs. Nothing wrong with a social club, but if Jesus wanted us to be a club, perhaps He would've used the metaphor that "the 18th hole shall not prevail against my putter."

Jesus chose the local church to be His conduit of hope for the world. Sitting and waiting for the world to come to us is not how Jesus imagined it. He told us to go. And as we go, the gates of hell will not prevail against us.

MARCHING ORDERS

Any person trapped in a situation that is not God's design for them is behind a hell gate. Imagine a child in Sub-Saharan

Africa whose village has no access to fresh drinking water. An evangelist comes to preach the gospel. The child is born again. But his drinking water isn't reborn; it's still putrid. In Ephesians 6:12, Paul referred to the "principalities and powers" that we wrestle against. An African child's country's principalities and powers tell him he's not valuable enough to have clean drinking water. The world system has overlooked him; there's no money in it.

James 3:13-18 tells us there are two wisdom types: wisdom from God and wisdom from demons. If it's not God's will, then it's a scheme of the devil. Does a child who has to drink filthy water oozing with bacteria and lots of other crap sound like God's wisdom? No way.

When the church comes together through the power of the seven to drill a well and provide clean drinking water for an African village, we are engaging the enemy on enemy territory. We are marching on the gates of hell. We are wrestling against principalities. We are deploying the power of the seven for the glory of God. The hellish gates of extreme poverty cannot prevail against the church.

Drug addiction in rural America, hurricanes on the Gulf Coast, or a global pandemic are all gates of hell stuff. As the church, God invited us to be part of the response of Jesus to the pain and suffering in this fallen world. But there's so much suffering out there. How can we know where we should go? There's more need than money; more challenges than hours in the day. Where do you start? God wrote the answer on your heart.

PASSION PLAN
In Acts 6, we discover that the earliest church in Jerusalem wasted no time in making sure they nurtured the widows in their community. There was no social program from the government, no safety net. There was just the church, and the

church stepped up. However, before long, a problem surfaced. There were Jewish and Greek widows, but the Greek women were left out. The church got together and appointed seven men, full of the Holy Spirit, to serve the Greek widows. (It's interesting to note that the church called seven men to serve. That integer may or may not mean that all seven gifts were present, but, once again, we see that number making a difference in Scripture.)

This story implies something else. Philip, Procorus, Nicanor, and Timon were among the men chosen. Why do I bring that up? Those are Greek names. Those were Greek men. They had a passion for helping the Greek widows and probably knew them. Those men joined forces to solve a problem that touched their hearts.

Which gate of hell should you attack? Well, what stirs your passion? Passion is healthy anger. I'm angry about what addiction does in people's lives. I'm angry about it because addiction almost stole my father from me when I was a child. I grew up poor and marginalized. It wasn't fair, and my anger about that creates a passion for helping those in extreme poverty in developing nations.

Passion is the fuel that will lead you to the gate of hell you need to attack with your gift. What makes you angry when you witness it? What breaks your heart when you see it? These are clues to where God is leading you. Frederick Buechner sums it up so perfectly:

> *"Whenever you find tears in your eyes, especially unexpected tears, it is well to pay the closest attention. They are not only telling you something about the secret of who you are, but more often than not God is speaking to you through them the mystery of where you have come from, and is summoning you to where, if your soul is to be saved, you should go next."*[10]

What makes you sad? In what way were you yourself comforted? If you're looking for the place to deliver your gift, I suggest you look no further than that. The Bible gives us wisdom in 2 Corinthians 1:3-4:

"Praise be to the God and Father of our Lord Jesus Christ, the Father of compassion and the God of all comfort, who comforts us in all our troubles, so that we can comfort those in any trouble with the comfort we ourselves receive from God."

You have been comforted in some specific way. Because of that, you have a unique opportunity to comfort others who are behind the same gate of hell you were once behind. A veteran with PTSD has a specific understanding of what that battle involves while I don't. If you've escaped from an abusive relationship, you've been comforted in a way that qualifies you to help others in the same situation.

BUM-RUSHING THE GATES OF HELL

There's no shortage of the seven gifts. I think the deficit lies in knowing what to do with them. It's not your fault; someone told you to sit still and shush. ("Sit down and be a good girl, and you'll get a treat on the way home from church.") It's not your mama's fault. But moving forward, let's not shush what Jesus wants us to shout!

In the Book of Ephesians, the Apostle Paul's language describes a well-equipped, highly trained, keenly focused army battling spiritual darkness. An army has many positions but one mission. Smaller units form to accomplish tasks that serve the primary mission. God explicitly equipped you for your mission. The weapons of our warfare are not carnal, but they are mighty. They have "divine power to demolish strongholds" (2 Corinthians 10:4).

Jesus invited us to follow Him into the mission of restoring what was lost in the Fall until He returns to fix everything. Maybe this is what it means to "be about my Father's business" (Luke 2:49). The members of the church are individually gifted to be about God's business. When a natural disaster unfolds, "Where is God?" is the most-asked question. The answer? He's right there in the church—where the individually gifted unite as one powerful force to rescue the perishing by bum-rushing the gates of hell.

Conduit Church has participated in numerous disaster relief efforts, including tornadoes in Joplin, Missouri, the 2010 Nashville Flood, and the massive earthquake that leveled Haiti.

In the trenches around us were people in their matching church t-shirts, operating together as the power of the seven to bring relief. Guardians were distributing supplies efficiently. Collaborators organized teams. Encouragers inspired everyone to keep going. Responders aided those who were suffering. Imparters navigated any conflict between team members. Visionaries scoped how challenges could be solved. And Discerners networked to raise funds.

As Peter told the church of his time, "Things have gotten bad." And when things get bad, the church has the opportunity to be at her best. The seven powerful gifts pack the church, but many are currently immobile, sitting still on pews, facing forward every single Sunday. Butt-stuck.

We must get moving! A group of Jesus people on the move—uniting their God-given gifts and acting like Jesus—is the church at its best. There is no time for sitting.

When Jesus said the laborers are few, He was right. When He spoke those words, there were twelve laborers. He told His disciples to pray that the Lord of the harvest would send laborers. And guess what? God did!

These days, the laborers are many, but we've utterly failed to communicate and understand the mission. Our gifts are butt-stuck on church pews!

Well, I'm blowing a horn! Laborers don't sit still! They are industrious and work shoulder to shoulder to get things done. Jesus' directive wasn't to send the laborers to fill up church pews but to harvest the fields.

Healthcare experts are increasingly saying that Americans are sitting too much due to our work and entertainment. Some say that sitting too much is the new smoking as a health hazard. Well, I'm here to tell you that sitting is killing the church. Immobility is not only hardening the hearts of believers; it's breaking the heart of God. It's time for the church to get on the move and change the world with the power of God's seven life-changing, world-shifting gifts.

Discover, develop, and deliver your gift, my friend. If you have a heart for addiction recovery, find Christ-centered ministries in your area and offer your gift to them. If your heart is for people to understand the Scriptures, homeless shelters, inner-city ministries, and crisis pregnancy centers have a spot open for your powerful gift. As someone who has operated a nonprofit for years, I assure you, there's always a shortage of workers.

If you're sitting in church waiting for permission to do something, you already have it. It's explicit in the mission Jesus communicated and implicit in the gift God gave you. Do you have a passion for serving single mothers and are gifted as a Collaborator? You don't need permission from anyone to start organizing a meal train or a diaper drive for a crisis pregnancy center. You don't even have to call it a ministry. As Bob Goff says, "Just call it Tuesday. That's just what people who are becoming love do."[11] You simply need to say *yes* to the prompting of the Spirit on the passion He imprinted on your heart and deliver your gift.

A Failure of Imagination

Reading this, you might be like I once was. I wanted to do something, but I didn't know what to do. So, I didn't do anything. It all felt so overwhelming, so big—and I didn't know where to start.

My failure wasn't of willingness; it was a failure of imagination. I didn't have any idea of where to go or how to start. I learned in those early days that God can't steer a parked car. So, my plan in its entirety was that I was going to start trying stuff. It had a little bit of the sense of a Jesus piñata—swinging and just hoping I hit something.

But God blesses feet that are moving: "How beautiful on the mountains are the feet of those who bring good news" (Isaiah 52:7). Note that it's not our ears or mouths that are beautiful; it's our feet. The feet speak of us moving forward, not sitting.

In 2005, Hurricane Katrina sledgehammered New Orleans. That crisis was the first time I can remember seeing something terrible happening and thinking, I really should do something. I was in my mid-thirties, a late bloomer.

My friend and music business colleague Jay Hall had put the word out that he was loading one of his semi-trucks with relief supplies to deliver into New Orleans. I thought, *Wait, you can do that? Can you just do something without having to ask or be told?* I didn't have language for it back then, but Jay Hall is a Visionary. He delivered a truckload of supplies, but he did something so much more in my heart. He awakened the possibilities.

Jay didn't know that's what he did for me. For him, that was just Tuesday. I'm so thankful for his leadership. I never again looked at a crisis the same way. Because of Jay's Visionary gift, I could see that Jesus gave us an incredible mission—if only I would get out of my seat and start moving.

What about discipleship, you ask? Not to be overly blunt, but what do you think discipleship is? Jesus said that a fully formed disciple would be like his master. What is a disciple? Someone who does and says what Jesus does and says.

Sermons are fine; I preach one every week. But fifty-two sermons in a year can't accomplish the world-shifting life change of working side-by-side with people for one week during their greatest need. When we do that, we are preaching with our lives. Discipleship is caught more than taught.

And what about evangelism? The church in action is just as good as any altar call Billy Graham ever gave. I could fill books with stories of people who came to faith in Christ because of the living sermon they experienced when the power of the seven brought clean water to their village. We don't require someone to be a Christian to participate in food distributions. We don't make them sit and listen to a sermon before they can eat. We simply move like Jesus right where they are. This isn't a new concept. Peter wrote about it 2,000 years ago.

The Bible tells us that we are foreigners in this land, and we should "Live such good lives among the pagans that, though they accuse you of doing wrong, they may see your good deeds and glorify God on the day He visits us" (1 Peter 2:12). I love the way The Message captures verses 11 and 12:

> *"Friends, this world is not your home, so don't make yourselves cozy in it. Don't indulge your ego at the expense of your soul. Live an exemplary life among the natives so that your actions will refute their prejudices. Then they'll be won over to God's side and be there to join in the celebration when he arrives."*

God doesn't want anyone to miss the party! And it's our job to haul in partygoers. In the next two chapters, you'll read real-life stories of the power of the seven in action. No one is sitting still in these stories. And believe me, the results are something to celebrate!

Chapter 16

The Seven Battle COVID-19

"For I consider that the sufferings of this present time are not worthy to be compared with the glory that is to be revealed to us."

– Romans 8:18; NASB

The Power of the Seven

In April of 2020, Tennessee's Governor Bill Lee issued the orders. To slow the spread of COVID-19 across our state, he closed businesses and schools, prohibited large gatherings, and instructed residents to stay home. Worldwide, there were two pandemics: one was microbial, the other spiritual.

In times of crisis, hospitals don't decrease their services, grocery stores don't stop selling food, and emergency responders don't shrink back. Neither should the church. History has shown that Christians run toward darkness, not away from it. In times of crisis, churches don't contract their services; they expand their impact.

During the pandemic's height, some media reported that churches were "closing their doors" all over the country. Nothing was farther from the truth. We weren't closing our doors; we were rushing out of them to seek and serve those who needed us. You see, Jesus didn't entrust the seven gifts to us so that we could go to church. He gave them to us with specific instructions: be the church, be His body, especially during hard times.

The Holy Spirit lays out the game plan for what we should do with our gifts during a crisis:

- Romans 12:13: "Care for the Lord's people who are in need." (Those in church family.)
- Romans 12:14: "Practice hospitality." (Those outside the church family.)

When Paul said the seven gifts are part of the "body" of Christ, he meant that the body should be implementing the ideas that the Head (Jesus) sends. At Conduit Church, we asked ourselves *During a pandemic, what ideas would Jesus want us to implement through the power of the seven?* Sure, we couldn't meet together on Sunday mornings for a while, but that was not such a big deal in the grand scheme. The power of the seven reaches far beyond walls.

THE WAR ROOM

To launch a power of the seven battle against COVID-19, our church staff began war-room-style meetings. Our church family members needed one another more than ever, even though the virus prohibited us from getting together. We also knew nimble, quick, and fluid actions were required. The situation was changing every day, sometimes every minute. So, we met the challenges we were facing head-on.

- The mandated quarantine demanded that we double-down on live streaming. But how could we create something that didn't look like an Osama Bin Laden ransom video?
- Of the 800 or so people in our church, we had folks rapidly losing their incomes. We needed to ensure that our church's most vulnerable—widows, single moms, and elderly living alone—didn't slip through the cracks.
- We needed to communicate effectively to our church body. That sounds easy given modern technology, but it's so much more challenging in many ways. There are many options to receive information, and different individuals prefer different methods.
- Urgent and time-sensitive needs were going to come up in our local community. We had to anticipate those needs and develop ways to meet them.
- Our friends in developing nations were going to be devastated by catastrophic loss. How would we continue to serve them, given COVID-19 restrictions and shrinking church funds due to job losses?

As the Discerner in that war room, my role was to view complex and disparate things and synthesize them to identify problems and solutions. But just because I'm good at discerning doesn't mean I'm adept at deploying the solutions. To battle this pandemic, we needed the seven powerful gifts firing on all cylinders. Prioritizing the needs, our team started with individuals who were part of our church family. That list consisted of 500 adults with needs. Conduit has less than a dozen people on staff, half of whom are part-time.

We felt that with the fear surrounding the coronavirus, a simple text message from us to those 500 individuals would be inadequate. We needed good old-fashioned heart-to-heart phone calls, which wasn't a simple task. How on earth would we make that many phone calls without overwhelming staff? Simple addition doesn't work to solve such a ratio imbalance. Ah, but God-math—multiplication through the power of the seven—does.

We had two goals: love people and our staff. To reach those goals, we deployed two Guardians and a Collaborator. Mo Thieman and James Boyd were the Guardians. My wife, Shannon, served as the Collaborator.

Shannon was the Zoom voice who wanted to ensure every person with needs was on the list. As a Collaborator, Shannon presses with her heart and pushes for us to do the hard things. She sees the physical needs and feels the emotional ones. Shannon spent the better part of a day looking at names and listening to her heart to solve the phone call problem. Then, she started collaborating, recruiting women who were seasoned prayer warriors to help make the calls. She broke down the hundreds of names into groups of twelve to fifteen individuals and assigned them to those women, staff members, and leaders who would also make calls.

James and Mo, steadfast Guardians on a mission, built and executed the call system and created the guardrails to maintain it. While Shannon saw the needs, those guys saw the practical applications of how a phone call project should play out—and just as important, how it could go wrong. They worked on the database to make it searchable and scalable. They built the tools to guarantee the information got from the right people to the right people. Mo adapted our database to accommodate notes for prayer requests and access from multiple people. James laid out a grid for small group leaders.

Within twenty-four hours, people were on the phones, and everyone in our church had been contacted and prayed for. As those calls were happening, we heard the specific needs of our church family: jobs were lost, people were sick, the elderly were isolated and alone. We had a benevolence ministry in place, but it was not scaled for a crisis of the size and scope of COVID-19.

And for that, it was time for the Responders. We have two of them on staff. Coincidentally, both are named David, and neither is interested in being called Dave. (While I can't prove it, there are ample clues that King David, not King Dave, was a Responder. But I digress.)

Based on Romans 12:13, we deployed those two Responders in separate silos. David Schindel led the ministry to those in our church family (give to the Lord's people in need). David Christopher led the ministry to those outside our church family (practice hospitality toward those who are not part of the church).

David Schindel deployed a team to dive into the complicated world of who needed what help and what Conduit's role would be in meeting those needs. This team included Imparters and Guardians, who were ready to assist with immediate financial needs and long-term financial planning. It also had Encouragers, gifted to embrace emotional and mental health care for those suffering from forced isolation. Team members needed the appropriate gifts to ensure we were helping and not hurting. But having a Responder leading such a diverse team ensured that there would be someone with the gift of mercy in the middle of it all.

David Christopher deployed his hospitality team—comprised of a beautiful mix of Collaborators, Encouragers, and Responders—to our local community. Their ministry encompassed everything from making face masks for medical professionals to visiting places such as laundromats to serve those in dire financial straits with no safety net. We needed someone in charge who was unfazed by obstacles and instead focused on getting it done. That was David!

David came alongside one of our Conduit members, Marion Ingram, a Collaborator, who had begun making face masks for medical professionals unable to obtain them due to a national shortage. He was the face of a ministry that was faceless. It seemed so apropos that those who were making the masks were primarily those in our church family who are generally unseen. The team was mostly women who had sewing skills, and the recipients were medical professionals who were working without the proper protective equipment. We had a group not generally in the middle of the action giving to people on the frontlines. It was a Responder's dream team.

Without a Sunday gathering, we needed to quickly ramp up an online broadcast as the primary communication, inspiration, and unification method for our church body. We deployed a Visionary and a Guardian.

Why that combination? Think of a Livestream as dual parts: What's created on stage and what's broadcast via the internet. A Visionary is the perfect gift to make sure what is going into the computer looks, feels and sounds amazing (camera, lighting, content). A Guardian is the perfect gift to make sure whatever is coming out of the computer is protected and distributed safely to the internet.

Keith Mohr, a Guardian, is a longtime friend, part of Conduit, and a former music industry colleague. Keith made sure that the content we created was broadcast to the appropriate platforms. He has the technical skills, but it was his Guardian gifting that ensured all the wires were connected, that the power was sufficient, and the different platforms were stable.

Although he wasn't on staff, we deputized Jim Cook, another Visionary, to handle the part in front of the computer. He has the skills needed to make it look amazing, but we needed more than his skills when battling COVID-19. We needed Jim's ability to see something that wasn't yet a reality. That's what Jim did as a Visionary. Jim didn't just drop in with a couple of iPhones on stands. He brought in cameras, lighting, and a portable studio. Our broadcast looked and felt amazing from day one.

Nashville offers an endless stream of options for music. Thankfully, we have Jason Kuhn, an Encourager, as our worship leader. One of my missteps was not having anyone leading worship on our first week of Livestream-only church. I had assessed that "Bob & Carol" sitting on their couch weren't going to "sing along." What this Discerner missed by a mile was that whether or not those watching were singing, Jason's mere presence brings encouragement. It helps that he doesn't suck as a music artist, but that talent is secondary to the gift. Point a camera at Jason, and by being himself, Jason loads courage.

What about the Imparters? We have three Imparters on our elder board. It wasn't on purpose, but it turns out to be an incredible bonanza! They are the thermometers for our church family. Jeremy Hezlep sensed our first week's broadcast was too jumpy and chaotic. Nobody else could've articulated that like a sensitive Imparter. The layout of the service itself was working against the content in the broadcast.

Initially, the layout of the service undermined our attempt to communicate peace and hope. So, we fixed that by week two.

It was the Imparters who also sensed the tone in the church family. Jim was pretty fast to deduce that men and women were experiencing the crisis quite differently. The men weren't coming across as afraid as the women were. It's not that the men weren't scared; it was that they weren't admitting it. The women, on the other hand, specifically the younger moms, were experiencing visceral fear. Imparters sensed all of that and worked gently and purposefully to mitigate it.

GLOBAL OUTREACH

As bad as the economic impact was in the United States, the devastation globally was incalculable. The UN World Food Program estimated thirty million people dying of starvation, not the virus. A lockdown in places like Uganda meant no public transportation, no work, and scant food. The slums of Guatemala and Kenya were locked down with no thought of how the people would survive. The virus would kill less than one percent of its victims, but starvation is 100 percent fatal.

How did the Conduit family know this? Because I'm a Discerner. I stayed in my lane reading, researching, and cutting through the fog to find the facts. My pastor friends were all receptive and willing to listen. They had not considered these implications. It wasn't because they aren't loving pastors but because they aren't Discerners.

I spent my days connecting with our partners in other countries, assessing the needs, and then working phones in the States to find folks who could help fund the initiatives. It was one moment on the phone with a special-needs orphanage in Guatemala that was out of food, money, and time—and the next emailing and bribing a communist police chief in South East Asia to allow our teams to distribute food.

Amy Roberts is the Guardian who kept me on the rails—categorizing donations to the right accounts, wiring the money, keeping track of the details. As fast as the money was coming in, we were sending it back out again. A two-thousand-dollar donation made on a Friday was purchasing food in Haiti by Monday.

We had boots on the ground in our partner nations; they just didn't have American feet in them. All borders and airports were closed, but the seven's power is not dependent on travel restrictions. In each country, we had Visionaries leading the way, Guardians stretching our dollars as far as possible, and Collaborators making distributions efficient and effective. Tens of thousands of lives were saved.

Before the pandemic, I had been feeling tired and worn down, but suddenly I felt energized. I didn't need a vacation; I needed a crisis. I was falling into bed exhausted every night, but it was the good kind of tired. The kind that you feel when you're who God created you to be.

LIVING OUT THE PROMISE

Of course, there were hiccups, tensions, and mistakes as we navigated ministry during the pandemic. Shannon, the Collaborator, would want to push too far; Mo and James, the Guardians, would not stretch far enough. And in the middle is the sweet spot. Collaborators and Guardians have tension, in much the same way an index finger and a thumb create tension. When they come together in the middle, that's where we find the most strength. Knowing the gifts in one another enabled us to see challenges not as conflicts to be avoided but tensions to be managed.

Conduit Church isn't a what; Conduit Church is a who. Whether it's an earthquake in Haiti, a tornado in Joplin, or a pandemic worldwide, we are Christ's body. We don't invite someone to "go to" our church. Our invitation is to join our mission of being the hands and feet of Jesus. We have seen Jesus do amazing things through us as we have humbly stepped in to deliver the gifts entrusted to us. We get to live out the promise of Psalm 133:1. "How good and pleasant it is when God's people dwell together in unity." Yes, the seven working together to deliver love and hope is a beautiful, powerful thing!

Chapter 17

The Seven in Uganda

"Declare His glory among the nations, His marvelous deeds among all peoples."

–1 Chronicles 16:24; NIV

K AWALIRA IS A TINY VILLAGE tucked between other small villages that spread across Uganda's African bush like a spilled box of Legos.® The people of Kawalira live in some of the most extreme poverty globally, and a lack of access to clean water has resulted in severe illness, sometimes death. Decade after decade, children there have had no access to education or opportunity, trapping them in a cycle of poverty. Life in Kawalira was nowhere close to "on earth as it is in heaven," until the power of the seven began to manifest.

Born and raised in Uganda, Alex Mitala embodies African wisdom. When he speaks, I take notes. When we're together, you'll often hear me say, "Wait, Alex, say that again! I want to write it down." You see, Alex is a Visionary on steroids—and where his vision goes, this Discerner wants to follow and learn.

As a young man, Alex pulled off a harrowing escape from execution by infamous dictator Idi Amin. His crime? Distributing Bibles. What does a Visionary do after narrowly evading death? Keep going. Soon after his escape, Alex began to lead a church-planting movement in Uganda that has outlasted not only Idi Amin, but multiple presidents, civil wars, and famines. The guy is impervious to the ups and downs of his country. When you can envision the future as clearly as Alex sees it, you keep going.

What did Alex, now in his sixties, envision thirty years ago that is now a reality? A school that boasts 2400 students annually. Thousands of churches planted all over East Africa. Tens of thousands of lives saved. A new generation of faith leaders raised up, trained by Alex, and advancing all over East Africa.

Alex was twenty years into this mission when I met him. I traveled with my eldest daughter, Madi, to spend a week with Alex in Uganda and see how Conduit Church could help. What did Alex do? He took us to empty fields and forests to reveal where new churches were planned. When Alex plants a church, he's growing life in a village. That church brings a clean-water well, a school, and a clinic—what Alex calls the four pillars: Christianity, education, healthcare, nutrition. Transformation follows as those pillars are grounded in a village.

When Alex took us to see Kawalira, it was a short tour. We popped out of the car, stood in one place, spun a tight circle, and then Alex said, "This is it." Madi and I stared somewhat perplexed at what Ugandans understatedly refer to as "the bush." Alex was pointing to where the church building would go, along with the school and clinic sites. He spoke as if those facilities already existed. All Madi and I could see were impenetrable thickets of trees and shrubs. But Alex saw them as if they were real. That's a Visionary.

At the time of our first visit to Kawalira, a scant eighth-mile long, a short strip of shacks doubled as markets for things like food, clothing, and alcohol. In the bush, hidden by trees and shrubs, people were living in little huts. They were tending gardens, cooking, and struggling to sustain life for another day. Witch doctors and shamans were active. There was a guy who thought he was Jesus. (Apparently, that Jesus needed multiple wives.) Women were doing backbreaking labor to keep their children alive one more day. Men tended cattle. All of this was sustained by whatever they could carve out of the ground, and drinking water hauled from a murky pond used for laundry, sewage, and livestock. And there were children, so many children. I think it's the children who keep the eyes of a Visionary like Alex focused on the future.

WORKING HAND IN HAND

In East Africa, church plants begin with a pastor who has been mentored and trained by Alex (or someone trained by him), walking alongside the Visionary for months on end. These men are Ugandan, and most have relational or ancestral connections to a village. Alex appoints and deploys the pastors and releases them to lead. For the village of Kawalira, that leadership is in the linked hands of Pastor Lawrence Lubega (an Imparter) and his wife, Eva (an Encourager).

After putting his trust in Jesus, Lawrence spent ten years working with Pastor Christopher Tamale, who was trained by Alex. When the time came, Lawrence accepted the call to plant a church in Kawalira. And this wasn't just any village. Lawrence was going home. He was born and raised in Kawalira.

Upon his return, villagers viewed Lawrence with suspicion—and for good reasons. Lawrence had once been a village drunkard. Jesus had transformed his life, but it took some time for locals to see him differently. It was his God-wiring as an Imparter—steady, calm, and unflappable—that gained their trust. In a village once marked by chaos, conflict, and uncertainty, Lawrence brought peace.

You don't have to speak the language of Lugandan to know that Lawrence's wife, Eva, is an Encourager. There might be a language barrier, but there's no gift barrier. People light up when they are with Eva. To the villagers of Kisagala, who for centuries couldn't see past the day at hand, Eva is the courage to see the future.

Five years after our first visit there, Kawalira now boasts a clean water well, a fully functioning medical clinic, a vibrant primary school, and a church building filled with hundreds of believers. Women who used to give their chickens to a witch doctor to remove a curse now keep them to feed their families. Children who used to die of something as simple as diarrhea now have access to the medicines most of us take for granted. Lawrence and Eva are still there, working hand in hand, imparting and encouraging. They are a modern-day Aquila and Priscilla, using their gifts and those of others to bring Kawalira closer and closer to "on earth as it is in heaven."

GLIMPSES OF GOD ON EARTH

Kawalira is one church among hundreds Alex has planted, and it's one of fourteen with whom Conduit partners in Africa. Like Kawalira, each village church has a similar story of impacting and changing countless lives. There's an enormous amount of complexity involved in this operation. To make things happen with integrity and effectiveness, the full power of the seven is on display.

Pastor Stephen Musisi is a Responder who has worked alongside Alex for almost thirty years. He oversees the social projects related to the planted churches. Stephen handles the heavy lifting of making sure those at risk receive the care they need.

Stephen performs his role without complaining and with a big smile on his face. Whether it's the work with Sudanese refugees on the northern border or the children in Kampala's slums, Stephen is on the front lines. He works with Alex in the central office and acts as the heart of the entire organization. When needs arise in Kawalira beyond the church's work scope, Stephen navigates those necessities with the mercy inherent to a Responder's giftedness.

Pastor Fred Manoga is a Collaborator who leads one of the churches with whom Conduit partners to make it a vibrant reality. While leading his church, Fred also orchestrates a trade school Alex launched to train people in skills they can use to provide for their families. It's not that Fred knows how to fix a motorcycle or operate a sewing machine or cut hair. It's that Fred knows how to recruit and deploy those who do. It's the perfect place for a Collaborator. This trade school is a gamechanger for countless Ugandans.

Jemimah Tendo is the Guardian who keeps everything on the rails. It's challenging to receive money from multiple sources and distribute those funds as designated. Conduit sends money to pay for teachers, classroom supplies, medical supplies, drilling wells, etc. If we send fifty dollars for a specific teacher's classroom and fifteen thousand to drill a village well, those funds need to get to the designated places. Donors entrust us to ensure this happens. The recipients' livelihood, and sometimes their very lives, depends on getting this right. Appointing a Guardian in this role protects this process. The wishes of donors are honored, life-giving water is delivered, and God is glorified—all because Jemimah is a Guardian gifted for it.

What about the Discerner in this endeavor? Well, I'm that guy. When teaching the Bible, my gift helps me connect the dots between ideas. In Uganda, my gift connects the dots between someone who has a need and someone who can meet the need. My role regularly includes connecting someone who has the finances and heart to provide clean water with someone who has no money and needs clean water. Insert healthcare, education, Bible teaching, and any other need you can think of, and that's what I do. I discern the situation and make the introductions. Because of that, millions of dollars have flowed to Uganda through our ministry.

Another aspect of my role in Uganda is teaching about the seven gifts. Students are not only learning how to read, write, and do math; they're learning who they are.

As I've said, the gifts are delivered through transformed Christians, whether they're aware of it or not. So why take the time to teach these things? Simply put, you should see the joy that fills the faces of Ugandans when they learn God has given them a gift; that He chose a gift specifically for each of them to deliver to the world. When they learn that the gift is not only in them but is them, it's a monumental moment.

Seeing the light go on inside someone is beautiful. When individuals realize they're not only a friend of God but a gift from God, it's stunning, and one of my favorite things.

When individuals experience this truth, it brings a sense of confidence and strength. And God is using these young men and women—with this truth downloaded inside of them—to change their villages and cities.

The power of the seven isn't confined to Western culture. The fact that these seven gifts can dynamically impact a culture historically gripped by poverty is a testament to the validity of what God has put in place. It's no coincidence the Apostle Paul first communicated the seven gifts to a church living in poverty while being persecuted by Emperor Nero. These gifts not only operate in hostile conditions, but they also thrive.

Part of the power of the seven is that these gifts flow whether or not individuals know it's happening. When you've submitted yourself as a living sacrifice, transformed by renewing your mind (Romans 12:1-2), you walk around being you, and your gift is delivered, whether or not you are aware of it. As I've traveled the globe extensively the past fifteen years, I've seen it firsthand. The power of the seven is active anywhere Christians are gathering. God is working to bring glimpses of Himself to earth. And it's a beautiful thing.

Thirty years after launching his vision for Uganda, Alex Mitala isn't resting on achieved goals. He can't help but see more. Visionaries keep envisioning; Alex is no exception. Even as you read these words, the work in Kawalira and countless other villages in Africa continues through the power of the seven. There is only one thing missing: you. I hope you'll consider my invitation to join me one day in Uganda, see firsthand the work God is doing, and deliver your gift there. I know some children who will receive you with enthusiasm.

Chapter 18

What the World Needs Now

"Our problem following Jesus is we're trying to be a better version of us, rather than a more accurate reflection of Him."

– Bob Goff

THE MAJORITY OF YOUR LIFE likely involves carpooling kids, going to the market, or providing for your family, not working with a team responding to a global crisis or solving a local problem. So, what do you do with your gift when all seven gifts aren't present? What do you do when it's Tuesday, and you're flying solo? Do you still have power? Absolutely! Why? Because of the power of love.

The Old Testament includes multiple names for God. It's not that God is a split personality; instead, each name is a representation of who God is. Likewise, each of the seven gifts represents a facet of who Jesus is. Delivering your gift is conveying a specific attribute of the character of Jesus. By being yourself, you're delivering a slice of Jesus. Here's a list of the seven gifts and the characteristics of Jesus they provide.

- Visionary: Patience
- Discerner: Temperance
- Collaborator: Goodness
- Guardian: Faithfulness
- Responder: Kindness
- Encourager: Joy
- Imparter: Peace

Do the words patience, temperance, goodness, faithfulness, kindness, joy, and peace sound familiar? You might notice they sound just like the fruit of the Spirit. And you would be half right. Galatians 5:22-23 tells us, "The fruit of the Spirit is love, joy, peace, forbearance, kindness, goodness, faithfulness, gentleness, and self-control. Against such there is no law."

You've likely read this Scripture passage a lot; you've probably memorized it. But did you miss its core truth? The word *fruit* in this usage is singular. The fruit of the Spirit is love.

The passage doesn't read, "the fruits of the spirit are..." Is the singular form of the word fruit a typo? I don't think so. I think it means that the fruit of the Spirit is love—and the other nouns listed, which we have called fruits, are descriptions of love.

Isn't that what Paul said in 1 Corinthians 13:4-7?

"Love is patient and kind. Love is not jealous or boastful or proud or rude. It does not demand its own way. It is not irritable, and it keeps no record of being wronged. It does not rejoice about injustice but rejoices whenever the truth wins out. Love never gives up, never loses faith, is always hopeful, and endures through every circumstance."

Those words aren't verbatim, but they do describe the authentic experience of love. To get what I am saying, think of love as an apple. The fruit of a Red Delicious apple tree is red, round, crisp, and tastes sweet. The fruit of the Spirit is love. It tastes like joy. It feels like peace and kindness with a texture of goodness. Galatians 5:22-23 describes the experience of the singular fruit—love.

I hope I'm not losing you because the reality of this passage about love gets even more awesome. There is a direct correlation between this statement about love and the seven gifts. Each gift brings a specific experience to the recipient. When you experience patience from a Visionary, goodness with a Collaborator, temperance from a Discerner, joy with an Encourager, peace from an Imparter, faithfulness with a Guardian, and kindness from a Responder, those delivered gifts are different aspects of love.

Don't miss this powerful truth! You aren't just delivering your gift; you're delivering the agape love of Jesus! What an honor and privilege! But here's the cool part: God designed you to deliver your unique aspect of agape love naturally by simply being you! He created you to love your neighbor as yourself. How simple is that? You don't have to morph yourself to match another's expectations or to make someone happy. That's codependency. Instead, delivering your gift requires simple dependence on God, the healthiest state of being.

In Jesus, we live, move, and have our being (Revelation 4:11). And that means being the true you. When you deliver your gift the way God wired you to give it, the people receiving it feel loved. It's as simple as that.

Mark Bourgeois is a Visionary who moves through life in the investment banking world with a sense of purpose and discipline. He has been incredibly successful. When Mark is in Visionary mode, he sees what others don't. Visionaries see the long run. They don't quit because they see what can be. That is patience personified. He asks incredible questions, and because of him, I gain clarity about situations. I feel less burdened. I can relax and patiently wait for what is to come because Mark, by being himself, has modeled the patience required to see a vision become a reality.

Audrey Cauthen is a Collaborator who leads the PreK ministry at Conduit Church. Audrey is good at what she does, but it's more than that. She does it with goodness. There's the uprightness of heart with which Audrey naturally handles every task and every person. When Audrey is in Collaborator mode, people experience the enveloping goodness of God.

Mike Howard is a Discerner and financial planner. During moments of economic crisis in our country, Mike can deliver his gift of wisdom into the lives of people who are facing scary situations. Financial markets are driven primarily by fear, and facts are the greatest weapon against fear. Mike's ability to look at the whole picture and analyze the facts brings a steady hand to the wheel in crisis. The Bible calls that temperance. An uncontrolled world needs the self-control of Mike the Discerner to steady us.

Phyllis Weil is an eighty-nine-years-strong Encourager. She still goes to work managing the books for her son's highly successful technology company. On Sundays, Phyllis doesn't volunteer in the nursery or make coffee or serve on the prayer team. What Phyllis does best is walk into the room and light it up with her gift. She's like a joy bubble machine! Phyllis often walks right up, kisses me on the cheek, and tells me I'm her favorite son. She moves through the room, being Phyllis, to everyone she encounters, and everyone walks away feeling uplifted. We walk away from Phyllis feeling like we can take on anything. Walk away feeling joy.

Jeremy Hezlep is an Imparter. He serves as an elder at Conduit and continually senses the general feel of what's going on in our church body. His gift provides keen insight into how we lead. By day Jeremy is the Director of Recruiting for Ramsey Solutions (Dave Ramsey) in Franklin, Tennessee. In both roles, Jeremy is a liaison. At work, he's the liaison between potential candidates and hiring managers. If you're a young candidate going in for your first interview, Jeremy has a steady and calming presence. If you're the hiring manager, Jeremy helps you see the whole picture and not just the candidate's nervous quirks. He stands in the middle and pours calm into a nerve-racking process. Jeremy brings peace to others because he is peace.

Amy Roberts is a Guardian who rocks at numbers, Excel spreadsheets, and balancing checkbooks. Most anyone can learn those skills. But Amy has the gift that shines in a Guardian: faithfulness. She's been handling the books at Conduit for almost ten years. Bookkeeper is her job title, and that's a perfect description of what she does. She keeps our books in the way you keep a family heirloom; she protects them. Millions of dollars flow into Conduit designated by donors to specific projects. These are people who are confident their gifts are safe with Amy. Her gift of faithfulness means people trust us. And trust is the primary currency of a nonprofit.

David Schindel is a Responder who serves as a pastor with us at Conduit. David lives in constant awareness of the needs of those around him. When others are in the hospital or crisis, David's gift compels him to go to them. He would go to those in need whether or not he was getting paid. The Bible talks about Jesus being "moved" with compassion. I can't think of a better description of David. I've watched him in action and have seen firsthand the God-given gift that reaches those in society who are down for the count or on the outside. Those who encounter David experience kindness.

My point in sharing this is to let you know that your gift is a conduit for Christ's agape love. A Guardian may think she is merely creating an Excel spreadsheet. Still, in reality, she delivers the gift of getting something done right—bringing faithfulness and safety to the process. That's delivering love.

"Beloved, let us love one another, for love is from God, and whoever loves has been born of God and knows God. Anyone who does not love does not know God, because God is love." (1 John 4:7-8)

God is love. God is good, kind, patient, faithful, gentle, peaceful, and self-controlled. The power of the seven gifts—used together or individually—rests in the ability to deliver God's love to the world around us. Whether that world is around the globe, across town, or down the hall, you are a conduit of love. The way God designed what feels so natural to you (because God created you to do it) feels supernatural to the person who doesn't have your gift. You have a supernaturally natural way to deliver love! How cool is that!

The Power of Love

"What the world needs now is love, sweet love." So goes the classic song by Jackie DeShannon. No truer words have ever been sung.

"Do you love me more than these?" That's the question Jesus asked of Peter when he was appointing him as a shepherd. Jesus didn't ask, "Do you *know more* than these?" or "Can you *do more* than these?" Or even "Are you *more capable* than these?"

Jesus wasn't herding His disciples into a competition for who could love Him the most. Instead, Jesus was giving Peter a glimpse of what He was asking of him as a Visionary. He wasn't turning Peter into a better version of Peter; He was transforming him into a more accurate reflection of Jesus. I love the way Bob Goff gets the important stuff:

"Our problem following Jesus is we're trying to be a better version of us, rather than a more accurate reflection of Him." [12]

Jesus, the ultimate Visionary, was deploying Peter to deliver that aspect of the *agape* love of Jesus to friends, family, and the world. The ultimate act of Jesus the Visionary reflected His view of the cross itself: "It was for the joy set before Him that He endured" (Hebrews 12:2). Jesus saw what was possible. But it wasn't the vision that propelled him; it was His *love* for us: "For God so loved the world" (John 3:16). Jesus was teaching that Peter didn't need more vision; Peter needed love.

Peter, like all of us, was on a long journey of transformation. Jesus loved Peter just the way He was, but way too much to let him stay that way. Jesus feels the same about you and me.

Peter got that message and spent his days on earth delivering his love-based Visionary gift. Inspired by the Holy Spirit and gleaned from a lifetime of following Jesus, Peter wrote these words near the end of his life:

> *"Through these he has given us his very great and precious promises, so that through them you may participate in the divine nature, having escaped the corruption in the world caused by evil desires.*
>
> *For this very reason, make every effort to add to your faith goodness; and to goodness, knowledge; and to knowledge, self-control; and to self-control, perseverance; and to perseverance, godliness; and to godliness, mutual affection; and to mutual affection, love." (2 Peter 1:4-7; NIV)*

Peter built the case for the fruit of the Spirit, saving the best for last by ending verse seven with "love." We, who have been forgiven much, can love much. The more we remember just how much Jesus loves us, the more we love others.

If I fail to communicate why love is so important, I'm afraid you'll put down *The Power of the Seven* and go out into the world with just another cool tool from a personality profile. But God's love for you is so deep and profound that He put a piece of Himself inside you. When you deliver that piece, free of shame or fear of rejection, the people who receive your gift experience God's love.

I wrote *The Power of the Seven* to awaken the possibilities of what can happen when the seven gifts come together powerfully. But I also want you to know that you can wake up on any given Tuesday and move through the world, delivering your gift wherever you are. There's miraculous power in that too. And love. Lots of love, which is what the world needs.

Chapter 19

You Have the Power

"So, since we find ourselves fashioned into all these excellently formed and marvelously functioning parts in Christ's body, let's just go ahead and be what we were made to be."

– Romans 12:6; MSG

A s he sat in a dark prison cell, did the Apostle Paul know the ripple effects of his obedience in delivering his gift as a Visionary? After all, Paul wrote the words, "Call those things that be not…as though they were."

Paul's vision for the church was not fulfilled in his lifetime. The prison where he lay shackled was under the rule of Nero—the Emperor of Rome and a psychotic nightmare. When Rome burned in AD 64, Nero concocted a plan to blame the Christians—and unleashed a wave of horrific persecution.

Paul was far from naïve; he knew his life was coming to an end. The only question was, how? Would beasts rip him into shreds in a Roman arena? Would he be burned alive and used as a torch to light the courts of Nero's palace? Crucified? Those were just some of the ways Nero tortured and killed Christians.

While sitting in prison, waiting to learn what Nero would do to him, Paul wrote the words we now know as the Book of Second Timothy. It's remarkable to me that in the environment of the unknown, Paul didn't focus on his discomfort, but on telling Timothy how to be a good pastor: *Don't put up with false teachers. Spend time in the Word. Watch your youthful lusts; they'll get you in trouble.* He was entrusting to Timothy the role of continuing with the vision God had given Paul.

Why Timothy? Why did Paul trust Timothy with a vision so vital? As Paul's protégé, Timothy traveled with Paul throughout many of his missionary journeys. So, it makes sense Timothy was on his radar. But it makes even more sense when you understand the personas of the seven gifts Paul described in Romans 12. Paul was handing his vision to Timothy, a Guardian, who would protect it even when Paul was gone. Paul recognized and respected the traits God had specifically embedded in Timothy.

Paul's Visionary gift saw the future and moved toward it. Even if it didn't include him, the future would include his gift. He delivered his gift until his dying breath and placed his vision into a Guardian's trustworthy hands. That was an early snapshot of the power of the seven working in unison.

Paul opened his letter to Timothy by challenging him to "fan into flame the gift that was within him." The awareness of everything that can go wrong—a characteristic of Guardians—can trap them in fear, paralyzing them. Paul opened his letter to Timothy by reminding him that God had not given him a spirit of fear, but one of power, love, and a sound mind. Doesn't that make so much more sense, knowing that Timothy was a Guardian?

And Paul didn't stop there. Even from his prison cell, he made sure the power of the seven was in full motion. By referring to what was happening all around him, Paul the Visionary showed that the seven gifts would continue to thrive without him. The church—for which he had plowed the path—would go on after Paul died. Don't miss how Paul in Second Timothy bolstered the enduring power of the seven that he described in Romans 12. In his last letter to the church, inspired by the Holy Spirit, Paul deployed the power of the seven through specific people:

The Responder: Onesiphorus

"Onesiphorus, because he often refreshed me and was not ashamed of my chains." (2 Timothy 1:16). I can't pronounce his name, but I can see Onesiphorus' gift so clearly. In 2 Timothy 1:7, Paul described him as "someone who searched hard for me until he found me." Paul was in prison—in danger and alone. His friend Onesiphorus risked peril to help Paul. That's what Responders do; they run toward those in danger, not away.

In the coming years, rulers would unleash even greater persecution on early Christians. Paul knew Responders would be needed. The mercy gift Onesiphorus gave to Paul was also given to many others.

Paul's prayer for Onesiphorus was that he would find mercy (2 Tim. 1:18). Responders are the gift of mercy, but they have the hardest time giving it to themselves. Paul saw that trait in Onesiphorus and prayed accordingly—but not just for the man. Paul was praying for the overall health of the seven. Each gifted member must understand individual strengths and weaknesses so that the church operates with ultimate power.

The Guardian: Luke

"Luke is with me." (2 Timothy 4:11). Is it any wonder that the one guy who was with Paul was a Guardian? It's believed that Luke was a scribe for much of Paul's writings, as well as for the story of Paul's ministry. Luke's visits to Paul in prison are most likely why we can read the Book of Second Timothy today. Not only is it probable that Luke physically wrote this letter for Paul, but that he also delivered it in person to the church. In the absence of email or a reliable postal service, a Guardian can be trusted to deliver a message safely and accurately.

Guardians are our protectors, and that includes protecting our stories. Because Luke used his gift well, we not only have Second Timothy, but we also have the Gospel of Luke, as well as the Book of Acts. Without Luke, the history of the early church would be lost forever. Luke protected it. That's what Guardians do.

Again, Paul was emphasizing how vital the seven gifts he wrote about in Romans 12 are for the growth of the church and the fulfillment of the prayer of Jesus, "Thy will be done on earth as it is in heaven." Paul the Visionary knew it would take a banding of all the gifts to get that job done.

The Imparter: Titus

"...and Titus to Dalmatia." (2 Timothy 4:10). Dalmatia was a region of ancient Rome. When you see Titus pop up in a letter from Paul or in Acts, it's almost always a conflict situation. When Paul departed Crete, he left Titus to bring order to what was unfinished. He sent him to Corinth when the conflict was brewing. Imparters like Titus brought resolution to skirmishes in the early church. There are no specifics about why Titus was in that region, but he served as the glue that held together the church located there—a church that would last for at least three centuries. In AD 302, Dalmatia was the epicenter for Rome's last wave of persecution against Christians. As sad as that was, it means a vibrant group of Christians still ministered there. Titus imparted his gift to a church that lasted for at least 250 years after his death.

The Collaborator: John Mark

"Get Mark and bring him with you, because he is helpful to me in my ministry" (2 Timothy 4:11). Twenty years earlier, Paul and his friend Barnabas had a huge falling out because John Mark had abandoned them on a mission trip. There's no mention of why Paul took such a hard stance, other than a younger and less mature version of Paul was angry and didn't want John Mark to come back. Barnabas (an Encourager), on the other hand, wanted to give John Mark a second chance.

I believe the power of the seven is one reason the relationship between Paul and John Mark eventually restored. Paul said, "He is helpful to me in my ministry." Helpful is a word synonymous with a Collaborator. As Paul learned throughout his ministry, a Visionary without a Collaborator is like a gas pedal without an engine.

Paul asked for his coat, scrolls, and parchments, which were in different locations. Paul needed them. Practical help is precisely where a Collaborator shines—and thus the request for John Mark the Collaborator. A critical request that involves moving parts in different locations with different people is a home-field advantage for a Collaborator. Paul needed those things, and John Mark did what Collaborators do best. He made it happen.

Encourager (Priscilla) & Discerner (Aquila)

"Greet Priscilla and Aquila." (2 Timothy 4:19). It's no small thing that Priscilla and Aquila are mentioned numerous times in the New Testament. They were a married couple who first met Paul when he arrived in Corinth, where they were exiled when the emperor banned Jews from Rome. Tentmakers by trade, the couple welcomed Paul into their business and home.

Priscilla and Aquila are always mentioned together in scripture and consistently described as "encouraging," and "teaching the Word." Paul mentioned them as greeting the church "heartily." Their home was always open. The descriptions of encouraging and hospitable don't naturally coexist with depth and in-depth study—unless one person is an Encourager and the other is a Discerner.

This power couple is named six times in the New Testament, and in four of the six instances, Priscilla's name appears first. At that time in history, women weren't given preference over men. For Priscilla's name to be mentioned first was a big deal. There's lots of supposition about why, but maybe it's just as simple as Priscilla was an Encourager. If you've ever been a close friend of an Encourager—or married to one—you have experienced how easy it is to be eclipsed by them. They're full of energy, life, and vitality. When they enter a room, they are noticed. Those hearty greetings to the church and encouragements to keep going were most likely the gift of Priscilla.

Which gift doesn't mind being overshadowed by anyone, including a spouse? That would be a Discerner, someone who naturally prefers being in the background, observing, and discerning what's going on. The ministry of Apollos grew when he was "shown more accurately" the way of God by his wife, Aquila. And he, in tandem, left others with a better understanding of God's ways. By using their individual gifts hand in hand, this married couple became foundational church leaders. Paul saw that coming!

POURED OUT

Even though Paul was in prison, his gift was not. The power of the seven was in full motion. As Paul's life attests, playing your role in the power of the seven does not guarantee a life of ease and comfort—or guarantee your safety. Living as one of the seven is not the ability to avoid crisis, but the power to go through it.

Some of Paul's last words stated that his life was being poured out "as a drink offering." An Old Testament drink offering was wine emptied on a sacrifice by the temple priest. The imagery is the priest holding up the vat of wine and pouring it out on the sacrifice. It was emblematic of wine for the Lord. Wine speaks of celebration, and this was God celebrating the forgiveness of His people. Pouring it out wasn't a waste of good wine; it was the symbol of God celebrating.

Paul's life, his Visionary gift, was poured out onto the sacrifice—held up by the great High Priest Jesus and poured out onto those whom Jesus had died to forgive. This truth is essential to understand. Paul pouring out his life in a prison cell could've been seen as such a waste of a good life. But the drink offering's image meant that Paul knew his life and gift were valued, not wasted. He was soon to be in heaven, being celebrated by his Heavenly Father.

Like Paul, you're pouring out your gift. Paul poured out his life to his dying breath. And you can too. Even if the people receiving your gift aren't grateful, even if you think no one sees it, keep giving it. The offering isn't for people. It's for the Lord. He looks at you and feels tremendous joy. The "joy of the Lord is your strength" isn't a command for you to pretend to be happy. Your Heavenly Father looks on you and feels joyful about you. His joy is your strength. The joy of an earthly father in his children bolsters and powers them forward. How much more does the joy of your Heavenly Father bolster and empower you ahead! Not a drop of your life is wasted. It all falls into the hands of your Heavenly Father as a celebration.

LIFTED UP

At the end of a championship football game, there's a celebratory moment when players pour a huge cooler of Gatorade® over the winning coach. And then, a player who worked hard to win the game is lifted up.

That tradition represents a glimpse of what happened when Paul stepped into eternity. The giant vat of Paul's life was poured over God. And then God cheered Paul, lifted him up and welcomed him home.

We all have a moment coming where we will pass from this life to the next. Imagine what it will feel like to hear God say, "Well done good and faithful servant; enter into your reward." And then the words of James 4:10 will be fulfilled: "Humble yourself, and you will be lifted up."

Where do you and I get the power to persevere on earth until we're lifted up in heaven? It all passes through the hands of Jesus. He will lift us up in heaven because He was lifted on the cross of Calvary. Jesus made the way clear: "If I am lifted up, I will draw all men unto me" (John 12:32). Jesus' life wasn't poured out as a drink offering; his life was poured out as a *sacrificial* offering. His sacrifice was accepted—and that is why there is something to celebrate! Because Jesus was lifted up on a cross, you and I can be lifted up into eternity.

Sure, there will be times when you don't think you can deliver your gift anymore. There will be days when you wonder if it's all worth it. There will be days when lions roar. There will be days when you feel alone and shackled. On those days, picture yourself asking Paul, "Was it worth it? Would you do it all over again?" Paul now knows the ripple effects of his obedience. He knows that nothing was wasted. For someone who has already enjoyed his victory parade, the answers to those two questions is an unreserved *yes!*

Someday, you and I will know the ripple effects of our obedience to deliver the gifts God placed in us. We'll see how those ripples extended into the years and centuries. We'll see how our Great Father intricately weaved together everything from beginning to end. We'll know that the joyous culmination is possible only because of Him. We'll join the great chorus of millions of fellow Christians singing the same song. We won't sing because we have to. We won't do it because we're robots. We'll do it because God really is that awesome!

Our astounding God chose to deliver some of His awesomeness through you. Remember, God had a plan and purpose for you long before you made your debut on earth. It's vital that you grasp your value in God's magnificent plan because you are important! It's a privilege for you to pour out your gift for Him and on those you meet each and every day.

By God's design, you're a living, breathing gift—and when you unite with the other gifted individuals in the body of Christ, together we become the answer to the most momentous prayer Jesus prayed: "Thy will be done on earth as is in heaven."

You are a vital member of the power of the seven, my friend, one-seventh of the solution to any problem. You are indispensable. Really, you are. Don't miss a minute of the phenomenal calling of God for the body of Christ. It's a dynamic way to live. And it can change you, your church, your community, and the world.

The power lives within you. So, put down this book and start delivering your life-changing, world-shifting life gift.

ACKNOWLEDGMENTS

Of all those who made this book possible, my family sacrificed the most. Shannon, in every way, this book is the result of your Collaborator's commitment, work, and life. It's beautiful to see you fully awakened and alive to the gift God has given you. Madilyn, as our firstborn, I learned so many parenting lessons on the job. These days, I gain knowledge by listening to and watching you move through life as a Discerner. Ben, you are a Guardian gift to my Discerner daughter. Thanks for aiming that gift at this book and helping me not look like a moron. Ashleigh, over and again, I've seen you be there for your friends in ways others aren't. I'm so grateful to watch God grow your Imparter gift. Whether it was on horseback or on a boat in Uganda, you have been a steady voice of calm and peace in my life. Lauryn, you've been protecting your siblings and parents since you were little, making sure somebody locked the doors and turned off the stove. As my Guardian girl, you always ensure we remember the small details that keep us safe. Ethan, God knew our family would be crazy enough to need two Guardians, and He gave us you. You keep us laughing with your wit and challenge us to think deeply. You keep me grounded and steady.

Mom, when I was a kid, you said I was going to be a pastor. All those conversations when I tried to change the subject were you protecting the calling you saw on me. Even though you didn't get to see me live that dream on earth, when we meet again, I look forward to hearing you say, "I told you so, Darren."

Dad, I see now that your Discerner gift is what shaped me. You taught me lessons about life that carved the man I am today.

Dale, Devin, and Don, as my brothers, you put up with a lot of crap from me. I'm just now learning that crap came from me not knowing and understanding my gift or yours. Thanks for not kicking me to the curb.

My mother-in-law Bonnie, it's comforting to know that, with you by Shannon's side and mine, at least someone will read this entire book.

Ivey Harrington Beckman, you dug this book out of me. Your Guardian gift has kept me on task and made sure these weren't just a clump of words, but a book people would actually read. You made this dream a reality, which isn't a platitude I take lightly. There is no way I could have written *The Power of the Seven* without you.

Nick de Partee and Ryan Dunlap, your design skills gave this book a personality and a place on the table. Thanks for helping this in-my-head Discerner put a printed book in people's hands.

Russ Rankin, we finally did it. We worked on a book together. Thank you for the hours you spent combing through the words and deleting the extra space after every period.

To the Elders of Conduit Church: Mo Thieman, "my right hand" isn't a strong enough title for you. You are my Guardian. Jeremy Hezlep, as a faithful Imparter, your peaceful stability has been key to my life and our church's success. Jim Henderson, you've been a firm shoulder, a steady hand, and a generous Imparter who has given life to me and our church.

Mark Bourgeois, as our Encourager, you didn't just see who Conduit was, but who our church family could become, infusing me with the courage to lead. Kyle Froman, you have been a steady voice of reason and calm from the start of Conduit, a Responder who has modeled mercy. Mike Howard, you're not afraid of questions, and as a Discerner, you ask even harder ones. For that, I'm forever grateful.

David Christopher, you have delivered your Responder gift to me and thousands of others here and around the world. From the jungles of East Africa to the coffee shops of Antigua you have showed up, and you stayed.

To my Conduit family: Our church isn't a what; it's a who. It's all of you. Together, we have seen God do amazing things. The power of the seven is alive and well in you.

Tony & Lynn Simpson, the Guardian duo. You wandered into Conduit when we were more of an idea than a church. You kept us and the vision safe. Shannon and I are eternally grateful.

Patsy Busey, you were my first pastor. Your Visionary gift bulldozed a path to a tiny town in the middle of nowhere and showed me a way that I couldn't see on my own. You saw the teaching gift in me when I was in sixth grade, and your Visionary gift is still alive and well in my life.

Dave Ramsey, you invited me into your world, asking for nothing in return. I wish the whole world could know the Dave I know. Sitting around the table in your basement propelled me to dream and step toward what is possible.

Jay & Pam Sekulow, you believed in me and Conduit when almost nobody did. Your Visionary gifts fought for us and beside us. Shannon and I are forever grateful.

Donald Miller, you inspired me with your Encourager gift without even knowing you were doing it. Your advice, encouragement, and example are why this book exists.

Dennis Rainey, your words "the 50s are the most productive decade of your life" stopped me dead in my tracks. When we got home from Europe, I started writing this book.

Michael and Cindy Easely, thank you for your friendship and inspiration. Much of my desire to "get it right" in this book came from your example.

Jamie George, there would be no Conduit Church if God had not downloaded courage from you into me. That courage has changed thousands of lives.

Jon Micah and Shannon Sumrall and my Kutless family, you kept me young and gave me gray hair at the same time. In many ways we grew up together. We learned together what faith can do.

Jon Courson, we've never met, but your teachings saved my faith and awakened in me the reality that became Life Gifts. If you ever read *The Power of the Seven*, you'll recognize some of the ideas and concepts that you have taught over the years. Thank you for delivering your Discerner gift to me and thousands of others.

NOTES

[1] https://marktwainstudies.com/the-apocryphal-twain-the-two-most-important-days-of-your-life/

[2] twitter.com/scottsauls/status1034143588899348481

[3] Fatina Hilal, *Curiosity Killed the Cat*, (Self-published: Amazon, 2014), Kindle.

[4] Brené Brown, *Braving the Wilderness*, (New York, NY: Random House, 2017), 40.

[5] Richard Evans, *Richard Evans' Quote Book*, (Salt Lake City, Utah: Publishers Press 1971), 244.

[6] Obituary of John Bisgno:http://www.kleinfh.com/memsol.cgi?user_id=2127097

[7] A.W. Tozer, *The Root of the Righteous*, (Moody Publishers, Chicago, IL, 1995, 1986), 165.

[8] C.S. Lewis, *The Lion, the Witch, and the Wardrobe*, (Harper Collins: New York, NY, 1950, 1978), 79-80.

[9] Aaron Niequist, goodreads.com/quotes/9457478

[10] Frederick Buechner quote source http://www.frederickbuechner.com/quote-of-the-day/2017/9/4/tears

[11] Bob Goff, *Everybody, Always: Becoming Love in a World Full of Setbacks and Difficult People*, (Nashville, TN, Nelson Books, 2018)

[12] Bob Goff, https://twitter.com/bobgoff/status/1018657430861856775

Made in the USA
Columbia, SC
19 January 2025